Jane Austen

GOODY TWO-SHOES.

By this means she soon got more learning than any of her play-mates, and
laid the following scheme for instructing those who were more ignorant
than herself. She found, that only the
following letters were required to spell
all the words in the world: but as
some of these letters are large, and
some small, she with her knife cut out
of several pieces of wood ten sets of
each of these:

a b c d e f g h i j k l m n o
p q r s t u v w x y z.

B 3   And

David Cecil

A Portrait of
Jane
Austen

Hill and Wang
New York

A division of Farrar, Straus and Giroux

First published in the United States of America 1979 by
Hill and Wang, a division of Farrar, Straus and Giroux

This book was designed and produced by
George Rainbird Ltd
36 Park Street, London W1Y 4DE

Picture Researcher: Philippa Lewis
House Editor: Georgina Dowse
Designer: Pauline Harrison
Indexer: Ellen Crampton

Text filmset by Jolly & Barber Ltd, Rugby, Warwickshire, England
Printed and bound by Dai Nippon Company, Tokyo, Japan

Library of Congress Cataloging in Publication Data

Cecil, David, Lord, 1902–
  A portrait of Jane Austen.

  Includes index.
    1. Austen, Jane, 1775–1817. 2. Novelists, English—
19th century—Biography. I. Title.
PR4036.C4   1978   823'.7 [B]   78–17317

(*reverse of frontispiece*) The History of Goody Two-Shoes
c. 1780 first belonged to Jane Austen who then gave
it to her niece, Anna Austen
(*frontispiece*) *Evening Dresses of the period*

To
Mary Clive

Good manners is such a part of good sense
that they cannot be divided.

George Savile, 1st Marquis of Halifax (1633–95)

Contents

Foreword

I must beg leave of my readers to preface this book with some words of explanation. First, it is intended neither as a straightforward biographical narrative of Jane Austen's life, nor as a study of her as author; but rather as an attempt, with the help of material drawn from her letters, her novels and other people's memories of her, to reconstruct and depict her living personality and to explore its relation to her art. Inevitably it is a tentative attempt; for, as I explain in the prologue, our information about her is fragmentary and her novels are none of them autobiographical. In order to make my picture clear and coherent, I have therefore been tempted to guess; and now and again I have yielded to the temptation. But I have done so as seldom as I could and I have been careful to make it plain when I was guessing.

Secondly, I have taken particular pains to set my heroine in the context of the period and society in which she lived. My reason for this is that I have come across critics who discuss her and her view of life and character as if they were those of a contemporary of their own. The result is a portrait comically misleading. For, as we should have learned both from social historians and common observation, we are all largely the creatures of the world we happen to have been born into and our outlook is conditioned by its assumptions and beliefs and conventions and customs. This is true to some extent even of rebels and eccentrics; it is outstandingly true of Jane Austen who was the very voice and typical representative of her world. Only in relation to it is she to be seen as she was. To be life-like, a portrait of her must also be a portrait of the society of which she was a member.

My third point concerns any passages in the book about Jane Austen's art. Those of my readers – I cannot imagine that there are many – who have read the Leslie Stephen Lecture on her novels which I delivered in Cambridge in 1935 may note that in these passages I repeat much of what I said in that lecture and sometimes in the same words. My excuse for this is that my views of Jane Austen's art have changed little since 1935; nor have I the ability to find new words in which to express old views. Inadequate though they may be, my old words are the best I can think of.

It remains for me to add some words of thanks: to Miss Philippa Lewis, for adding greatly to the interest of my book by collecting and helping to select its illustrations; to Miss Elizabeth Jenkins and Mr Brian Southam for the invaluable light they shed on my subject by their writings; to Mrs E.M. Rose for her kind help to me on my visits to Chawton Cottage; to Lord Leigh and to Mr Walter Serocold for their courtesy in allowing me to see over Stoneleigh Abbey and Ashe House respectively; to Miss Helen Lefroy and to Commander Francis Austen and his brothers for allowing me to reproduce in my book many pictures from their collections.

David Cecil

A Prologue

The World

Appropriately enough, it was on a visit to an eighteenth-century country house that I first made the acquaintance of Jane Austen. There, in its drawing room, with the portraits of powdered and beruffled ladies and gentlemen staring down at me from the faded silk of the walls and the tall windows open onto stretches of parkland hazy in the light of a fine September evening, my mother opened *Pride and Prejudice* and began to read it aloud to me. She went on with it during the days that followed. By the time she had finished, I was wholly under the spell of the author. This happened well over sixty years ago and the spell is still working.

During the interval I have read *Pride and Prejudice* and Jane Austen's other books many times and my appreciation of them has widened and deepened and, I suppose, grown more discriminating. I have learned to recognize their limitations and occasional weaknesses. But I delight in them just as much as ever; perhaps more. From the first I found them irresistibly amusing; now I have come to recognize them as penetratingly true pictures of human life and artistic achievements of a Mozartian perfection.

Pleasure in art is not the same thing as interest in artists, and it was not until much later in life that my response to the spell led to curiosity about the spell-binder. Then I did begin to wonder what kind of woman Jane Austen was. From such evidence as remained to us, I sought to find out. As a result of my researches, came a desire to try my hand at painting a portrait of her. I realize I am not the first in the field. Others, notably Dr R. W. Chapman and Miss Elizabeth Jenkins, have preceded me. But after all, the fact that Romney painted several pretty portraits of Emma, Lady Hamilton, did not stop Sir Joshua Reynolds from adding to their number. In spite of Dr Chapman and Miss Jenkins, I decided to have a try, and all the more because their portraits, though convincing, were not complete enough to be final. Indeed they could not be. Nor, as I was to discover, could mine. Fate and man between them seem, almost deliberately, to have conspired to keep Jane Austen's figure at a distance from posterity. The actual facts of her life tell us little about her. She was born at a period and in a class whose life – quiet, sheltered, strictly bound by convention – was likely to be uneventful, especially for women. Certainly nothing dramatic seems to have happened to Jane Austen; nor have we any continuous account even of its undramatic incidents. Our information about her is drawn mainly from her letters to her sister Cassandra; but for a large part of the time Cassandra and she were together and had no need to write to each other. In consequence, months, sometimes a whole year, of her story went by almost unrecorded.

Further, these letters are made up mostly of family news, neighbourhood gossip and practical talk about dress and household management. They contain few of their author's thoughts and fewer of her confidences. Here it is that man has intervened to help Fate keep her at a distance from us. Cassandra disliked the idea of posterity prying into her sister's history and especially of learning about anything in it she might have wanted to keep secret; so, after Jane's death, she destroyed any reference in her letters to any event or phase of feeling that, in her view, had seriously disturbed the even tenor of her sister's days.

Cassandra's action has, naturally enough, disappointed Jane's biographers. But I have come to doubt whether they have lost much by it. It is unlikely that her letters, even if preserved in full, would have been very revealing. For one thing Jane Austen was brought up in a family which – to judge by their correspondence – were noticeably discreet and reticent. For another, there are signs that she was by nature disinclined to talk about herself. The subject does not seem to have interested her.

This lack of interest showed itself in her work. There are novelists – Charlotte Brontë and Proust are examples – whose books are largely auto-biography. They employ the novel form, he to analyse his experiences, she to unburden her heart; and both in a manner so little disguised that we are justified in using their books as evidence, when investigating their life stories. But not all novelists are thus self-inspired. There is another kind whose eyes are turned not inwards but outwards; it is what they observe in the world outside which stimulates their creative impulse. Further, these observations are as objective as they can make them. Of course, their stories will inevitably be coloured and shaped by their point of view and characteristic mood. But only implicitly and because they cannot help it; they are not consciously concerned with themselves and they do not want their readers to be concerned with them either. Scott and Trollope are examples of this type of writer. So also and outstandingly is Jane Austen. She never tells a story in the first person, she cannot be identified with any of her heroines and, so far as we know, no incident or character in her books is drawn direct from life. It may be noted that she took care not to have her novels published under her own name: they were described on the title page 'By a Lady'. No doubt in this she was following a convention; born and bred a lady in the purely social sense of the term, she may well have felt it unseemly to present herself, as it were in person, before the public. But there is surely a deeper significance in her anonymity. It was a testimony to her sense of her art as something apart from her private self. Her novels were not personal revelations and she was determined not to give her readers any opportunity to treat them as if they were. It is no use going to Jane Austen, the novelist, for direct and factual information about Jane Austen, the woman.

Nor do we get much help from the people who knew her. She did not live among memoir writers and personality-fanciers; besides, since she published nothing till after she was thirty, nobody who knew her during the early part of her life would have thought her worth taking special note of. Many years later, when she was dead and famous, those of the younger generation of her family who remembered her did write down some of their memories. These give us a lively impression of her figure as it appeared in the family circle, they help us to imagine how she talked and visualize what she looked like. But they show her to us only during the last two or three years of her life; and as she appeared to girls and boys in their teens, too young to be in her confidence or even to guess anything about her inner life.

No – as her would-be biographer, I had to face the fact that information about Jane Austen the woman was limited and fragmentary. She remains for me – as no doubt she would have wished – not an intimate but an acquaintance. All the same the temptation to try my hand at drawing her likeness was not to be resisted. Some people are well worth knowing even as acquaintances. Jane Austen is one of them. She reveals herself in her letters and records as a personality with a sharp, subtle, agreeable flavour of her own; a personality observant, perceptive, amused, perhaps formidable, certainly intriguing and all the more so because she seems very different from the conventional idea of an author of genius.

II

Indeed, she was in most respects startlingly unlike most authors of genius. In particular she differed from them in that she was at ease in the world she was born into. Several things account for this. In the first place the countryside of southern England, where she spent most of her life, was a pleasing and reassuring region, with its green smiling landscape of field and woodland and

Family life in eighteenth-century England: reading and writing. By John Harden

leafy hedgerows, of spacious skies and soft horizons; and with something at once homely and immemorial in the atmosphere emanating from its thatched villages, each centring around a grey old church, its interior enriched with sculptured monuments of successive generations of local landowners and set in a grassy churchyard populated by gravestones inscribed with the names of successive generations of their tenants; and the two combining to suggest an extraordinary feeling of social and family solidarity and continuity.

For the poorer villagers no doubt there was another side to the story: their life, though relatively secure, was a hard one. But Jane Austen was not a villager but a child of the gentry; she came from the world of squires and better-born parsons, of naval and military officers and the fellows of Oxford

and Cambridge colleges. The gentry were seldom rich as were the great
nobles of the day whose palatial residences were so conspicuous a feature of
the rural scene. But, for the most part, they were comfortable enough; and, as
much as the nobles, they were members of the ancient established ruling
classes of England and treated with the respect and deference due to them as
such. Moreover their form of life, though limited and monotonous by
modern standards, was peaceful, comfortable and leisurely, free from anxiety
about its future, worrying little about politics and world events.

Their confidence was strengthened by the spirit of the age, the eighteenth
century. It is necessary particularly to stress the century, in spite of the fact that
Jane Austen lived nearly half her grown-up life after 1800. Country life
in every age tends to trail behind town life and especially in those days when
there were no telephones or radios or daily posts and the horse was the fastest
means of travel. Moreover, the country gentry, alike in their habits and their
views, were a conservative-minded body. Jane Austen – it is one of the most

'Music', by John Harden

important facts about her – was born in the eighteenth century; and, spiritually speaking, she stayed there. A contemporary of Coleridge and Wordsworth, her view of things had much more in common with that of Dr Johnson.

This was not a disadvantage to her. There is a great deal to be said for Dr Johnson's view of things. Indeed, provided one was born English and in sufficiently easy circumstances, there was a great deal to be said for living in the later eighteenth century. Existence then was characterized by a blend of qualities that gave it a peculiar amenity. This blend can still be seen in the productions it has left to us. Its domestic architecture for instance; not so much the grandiose mansions inhabited by the nobles as its more modest manifestations, the smaller country houses where the squires lived, the roomy rectories which housed the parsons; or, in towns, the residences which compose the squares and crescents of Bath and Edinburgh New Town. All these are eminently practical structures, rationally designed and solidly built. But they are also graceful and mannerly, with their well-proportioned exteriors of grey stone or rosy brick, their white-painted woodwork, their sunny sitting rooms small or spacious, their bedrooms gay with striped wallpaper and flowered chintz; while interior and exterior alike are dignified by an unobtrusive unfailing sense of style, apparent in their symmetrical façades, the delicately wrought fanlights surmounting their front doors, their chimney-pieces ornamented with urns and garlands. A sober English variation on a classic theme, these houses contrive to be at once friendly and stylish, elegant and livable.

The same is true of their furnishings. A Chippendale chair is as comfortable to sit on, a Sheraton writing desk as convenient to write at, as are their modern counterparts. But, unlike these, they are also charming works of art, their fine simplicity of line enriched by an occasional touch of decorative carving or by a surface of subtly varied veneers. So also is a teacup of the time – grey-blue Wedgwood or rose and gold Worcester – both pretty to look at and easy to drink out of. Like the houses and the chairs, it does equal justice to the claims of the useful and the agreeable.

As such, it reflects the ideals of the society which produced it. This meant one that seemed, at any rate, to be settled and secure. With the Glorious Revolution of 1688 and the accession of the House of Hanover, the fundamental issues, political and religious, which had torn England in two during the sixteenth and seventeenth centuries had been decided and in a spirit of relatively reasonable compromise; and, though this did not stop the various factions in church and state from still going in for a good deal of high-spirited squabbling, no one was prepared to carry this to the point of risking another civil war. Nor was any new fundamental issue to trouble the nation till the rise of the democratic movement. This however was not till the last years of the century. Eighteenth-century England, so far from being democratic, was a hierarchic society run by a hereditary oligarchy of nobles and squires, in which everyone, high or low, accepted distinctions of rank as part of the natural order as ordained by God. But, like the religious and political settlements, these social distinctions were not extreme or inflexibly enforced – people had a chance of rising and falling in the social scale – and their effect was further modified by a feeling of national solidarity common to all classes. It was an age of militant patriotism. The aristocracy did go in for a certain amount of cosmopolitan culture: they quoted Latin poetry and bought Italian pictures and sent their sons abroad to finish their education on the Grand Tour. But, as much as their social inferiors, they took for granted that Englishmen and English institutions were unquestionably superior to any others in the world. 'Rule Britannia' is an eighteenth-century song; and, alike in the genial arrogance of its words and in its florid triumphant tune, it well expressed the eighteenth-century Englishman's attitude to his fatherland.

> Rule Britannia, Britannia rule the waves,
> Britons never never will be slaves.

The English of the eighteenth century sang these words with a pleasant certainty that the same claims could not be made by benighted foreigners on the other side of the Channel.

National self-confidence was the expression of national character. This was vital, tough, vigorous and enterprising. The end of the struggles of the previous age, so far from leaving the English exhausted, only released their energy for other things. These – in contrast to the activities of their fathers and grandfathers – were less ideological than practical. Having come to some sort of working agreement as to the nature of the society they were to live in, people turned their attention to investigating its characteristics and to improving its workings; and they did both in a spirit that aspired, at any rate, to be cool and reasonable. Some concerned themselves with scientific inventions and the development of trade and industry and agriculture, others with studying the human scene and noting and classifying its varieties.

For – and here again in contrast to their parents and grandparents – they were less concerned with man in relation to God and his own soul than with man as a member of society and in relation to his fellows. Man was primarily regarded as a social being and judged by his conduct as such. The standards of judgment employed were distinguished mainly by two characteristics. The first was its realism. A belief or an action was valued in so far as it did in practice contribute to the well-being of mankind; and this involved as a first and necessary step facing the basic facts, physical and material, of human existence. Eighteenth-century England faced them robustly and with its feet firmly planted on the earth. For example, it realized that man had his carnal passions, though he should learn to control them; also, even if it were wrong to sacrifice principle for money or for social position, it was foolish to pretend that these things were undesirable. To refuse to recognize this would show a lack of good sense. 'Good sense' was for them a phrase of the highest commendation.

Further, realism and good sense between them taught the harsh lesson that life was incurably imperfect and that it was a sign of weakness to hope too much from it. Or to fear too much either; people believed profoundly in moderation and balance. The frenzies and fanaticisms of the seventeenth century had shown them that extreme views led to uncomfortable results. Also to ridiculous ones; this last was to men in the eighteenth century an important consideration. Its clear breezy climate of good sense and self-confidence made it an age in which humour flourished. For the most part it was ironic humour. Realists are quick to note any comical difference between pretence and reality, between truth and day-dream; and to enjoy it. These realists enjoyed it wholeheartedly; for they were seldom so tender-hearted as not to get all the fun they could out of what struck them as absurd. Their irony varied in flavour: stately in Gibbon, whimsical in Sterne, bitter in Swift. But on the whole, eighteenth-century irony and eighteenth-century humour in general – though not particularly kindly – was high-spirited and cheerful.

This did not mean flippant or irresponsible. On the contrary its social concern made eighteenth-century England firmly moral. 'Respected for his many virtues and his constant attention to the duties of his station' – how many memorial tablets of the century are graven with this or similar in-scriptions! The virtues and duties here implied are, as was to be expected, social ones: benevolence, prudence, honesty, public spirit. It is to be noted that these tablets are to be found on the walls of churches. Though it had reacted against the fanaticism of the Civil War period, the English eighteenth century was far from irreligious. The average educated citizen was an orthodox believer and a regular church-goer, who, if he felt disposed to do a little serious reading, might turn to a book of sermons, as people nowadays might turn to a biography. A reasonably large number of persons were actively pious, as the spirit of the age counted piety. A good Christian, in its view, was a man who did his duty in that state of life to which it had pleased God to call him and this meant duty to his fellow men; as master or servant, neighbour or citizen, parent or child. Family duties were especially emphasized; for the family was the nursery of social virtues, the divinely ordered, natural unit around which a coherent society was built and maintained; and marriage, though not necessarily a romantic affair – to marry purely for 'passion' was looked on as irresponsible – was for the eighteenth-century Christian an institution involving lifelong and serious obligations. Parents and children also were united by a bond involving serious obligations on both sides. For the rest, the eighteenth-century Anglican was seldom interested in theological speculation and was sceptical about mystical visions. Unbridled religious emotion – what was then termed 'enthusiasm' – was regarded with especial suspicion. 'Enthusiasm' was a term of abuse as 'good sense' was a term of praise.

Good sense also worked to discourage religious people from being puritanical. Mrs Thrale once quoted to Dr Johnson a line written by Garrick expressing the wish 'to smile with the simple and feed with the poor'. Johnson was not impressed. 'Nay, my dear lady, this will never do,' he said, 'smile with the simple; – what folly is that? and who would feed with the poor that can help it? No, no: let me smile with the wise and feed with the rich.' Johnson was a devout Christian, but this did not mean that he felt guilty about enjoying a good dinner, or amusing himself in intelligent company; he wanted to 'smile with the wise'. Here we come to the second distinguishing characteristic of the eighteenth-century point of view. In addition to being realistic, it was civilized. 'The man of sense' was all the better for being also a 'man of taste'. Taste implied learning and discrimination; learning and discrimination were acquired by a thorough grounding in the established and classical tradition of scholarship and the arts. This grounding combined with the virile vitality of the age to produce a strong fresh culture; in thought and architecture and painting and literature.

The nature of this culture was conditioned by the general outlook of the age. It was social and practical. Its most characteristic buildings were dwelling houses; its best pictures, portraits and scenes of contemporary life; its most typical books, novels and biographies and satires and essays, works describing and commenting on the world of men and women that the authors saw around them. Further, they were designed to appeal to the interests and feelings and taste of the general reader. Johnson praised Gray's 'Elegy in a Country Churchyard' because it 'abounded with images which find a mirror

Watercolour sketches by Cassandra Austen of Mary Tudor,
Edward IV, Henry V, Mary Queen of Scots, Elizabeth I, and Charles I,
for Jane Austen's History of England *c. 1790*

TUOUS LIQUORS

WINES

Hackney Coach.

& Etched by J.A.Atkinson.

in every mind and with sentiments to which every bosom returns an echo'. Pope said poetry should be: 'What oft was thought but ne'er so well expressed'.

For him and his readers 'well expressed' meant intelligible on the one hand and on the other agreeable. Nor was it only poetry that should be agreeable. Eighteenth-century ideas of culture applied to the art of living as well as to the art of writing; and much time and energy was spent in cultivating it. Private life flowered as never before in English history; so also the modes through which it expressed itself, the arts of conversation and of letter-writing. Manners were looked on almost as an aspect of morals; politeness almost as a virtue. Concern for politeness was, like everything else, checked by realistic good sense. The eighteenth century mocked mercilessly at the affected and precious; and, even at its most moral, it was not squeamish. Its talk was racy as well as polished. It could enjoy eccentrics if they were entertaining; it forgave Johnson his uncouthness for the sake of his wit and his wisdom. Like its houses and its chairs and its teacups, social intercourse in eighteenth-century England was the expression of a society that, at its best, managed to be at the same time both sensible and stylish.

It took time to reach its best. England in the first half of the century – the riotous, brutal, uproarious England depicted in Hogarth's pictures and Smollett's novels – was far from civilized in any high sense of the word; and some of its less pleasing characteristics were exhibited even by the people who sought to civilize it. Good society, as portrayed in Pope's poems and Lord Hervey's memoirs, was sensible and stylish all right; but its good sense could be disagreeably harsh and earthbound and its glittering stylishness went along, all too often, with insensitiveness of feeling and a hard-hearted worldliness.

As the years passed these things began to change. Various movements helped to accelerate this change. The Evangelicals, led by Wesley and White-field, preached a more fervent piety and stricter morals; Sterne and the apostles of sensibility introduced a new object of admiration in the shape of the Man of Sentiment who exalted fine and sympathetic feelings at the expense of cold reason. Meanwhile, in the realm of taste, came a reaction against too rational and classic an ideal. William Collins sang the beauties of wild nature; Horace Walpole had his house decorated in the 'Gothick' style. Evangelicals, Sentimentalists, lovers of nature and 'Gothick' were all in their different ways and degrees out of sympathy with realistic moderation and, as a result, came in for a good deal of mockery from the conservative-minded

Hackney Coach

majority who did believe in it. This did not however stop people gradually responding to the new influences. That of the Evangelicals was felt mainly among the middle class; it worked towards a greater outward decorum. The feeling for nature and the Gothic affected the higher ranks of society; it would be misleading to say that it improved their taste – early eighteenth-century taste was admirable of its kind – but it made it broader and more varied. Finally, the Men of Sentiment did a great deal to encourage any tendency towards more humane views and more sensitive feelings.

The consequence of these various influences made its appearance in the last quarter of the century. In art Gainsborough, not Hogarth, now mirrored fashionable taste; young people with a liking for poetry preferred reading about Cowper's walks in the woods to Pope's observations on the follies of fashionable ladies; landowners, anxious to beautify the grounds of their country homes, employed Humphry Repton to replace formal gardens by parks artfully planted to look like works of nature. A similar change of taste showed in the way people dressed. Men began to wear their hair curled but unpowdered, women to discard stiff hoops in favour of elegantly flowing skirts. These alterations in taste were the expression of an alteration in manners. Gentlemen swore and drank less – though still a great deal more than they were to do a hundred years later – some even began to question the moral rightness of duelling. Both sexes talked less coarsely. 'Delicacy' became a popular word of praise. In 1700 persons of the highest quality delighted in Congreve's *Love for Love* as an example of comedy at its finest; in 1778 Fanny Burney found it so indelicate as to bring a blush to the cheek of any well-brought-up young lady.

As always, the town was the first to exhibit these changes. But the country soon followed and the later eighteenth century saw the life of the country gentry noticeably more civilized than that of their grandparents. Gone were the *naif*, ignorant Squire Sullens and Squire Westerns of sixty years earlier, with their rustic accents and oafish manners; to be succeeded, as often as not, by educated gentlemen who, as well as hunting and shooting and sitting on the local Bench as magistrates, collected libraries and interested themselves in new developments in agriculture. A similar change had happened to the country parson. In 1720 he had sometimes been hardly better than an upper servant, born in a lower rank of society and who took his pleasure drinking with the Squire's butler. By 1790, he was likely to be one of the Squire's relations – perhaps a younger son – who had been at the university and who combined life at a well-appointed modernized parsonage house with an occasional day's hunting and some weeks' social enjoyment in London or Bath.

This growing refinement of manners went along with the growing social influence of women. Of course, in high society women had often been influential, even formidable; the names of Sarah, Duchess of Marlborough, and Lady Mary Wortley Montagu are enough to remind us of this. But these names suggest that they were powerful in virtue of what are generally looked upon as masculine qualities: masterfulness, aggressiveness, force of personality. In the later eighteenth century, growing refinement of feeling and taste led to women exercising influence by their characteristically feminine qualities and talents: intimacy, imaginative sympathy, graceful manners. Moreover with the flowering of social and private life these had more scope to display themselves than earlier. Always, in so far as a society cultivates social pleasures and sets store by the private life, women grow powerful. Women rule private life as men rule public. So it was in the late eighteenth century in England. This was the period when English aristocratic society was at its most agreeable; these were the days of Devonshire House and Holland House and their brilliant hostesses. In the professional classes, also, women's influence grew strong. Dr Johnson may have shown himself at his most trenchant in the all-male society of the Club, but it was in the company of Mrs Thrale and Fanny Burney that he was at his happiest and most relaxed. At the same time, women's intellectual position became more important. It was now that the phrase 'blue stocking' was coined to describe such formidable ladies as Mrs Montagu, the Shakespearian critic, and Miss Anna Seward whose poems had earned her the name of 'The Swan of Lichfield'. Fanny Burney herself is the first female novelist to achieve the rank of a classic. This growth of female influence was yet another element helping to modify the characteristic eighteenth-century ideal. For, by the end of the century, it had modified noticeably to present itself in a version, refined, subtilized, and with the coarser, harder strain, which disfigured it in the days of Pope and Lord Hervey, at best softened and at worst decently concealed.

Yet the basic essential character of that ideal had not changed; and it still commanded the adherence of the majority of educated people. Understandably too; and especially in its latest, most civilized manifestation. It is a satisfactory society and a rare one that succeeds – if only occasionally and in part – in combining good sense, good manners and cultivated intelligence, rational piety and a spirited sense of fun.

Certainly it suited Jane Austen.

I

The Family

It suited her relations too. On both sides she was descended from well-established respected families of squires and parsons. Her father, George Austen, had, it is true, started life in circumstances less than genteel. William, his father, a younger son with no fortune of his own, earned his living as a surgeon – not in those days considered a gentlemanly profession – and both of George's parents had died before he was nine years old leaving him a penniless orphan. However a benevolent wealthy lawyer uncle, Francis Austen, took pity on him and paid for his education at Tonbridge School. He was a clever boy; and he proceeded thence as a scholar to St John's College, Oxford, where he later became a Fellow. He had matured into a young man who, in every respect, was a credit to his Uncle Francis. On the one hand he was an accomplished scholar well read in several languages and with a fine taste in literary style, on the other he was an agreeable social figure, unusually good-looking – he was nicknamed 'the handsome Proctor' when a don at Oxford – with bright hazel eyes and thick wavy hair, and possessed of an easy hopeful temper and pleasant manners. These intellectual and social advantages won him the favour of another rich relation in the shape of a distant cousin called Thomas Knight, a landowner with property both in Kent and Hampshire and who lived in a big mansion, Godmersham Park near Canterbury. Learning that George Austen wanted to become a clergyman – George added piety to his other virtues – he presented him with a living of which he was patron at Steventon, a little village near Basingstoke. To this, his Uncle Francis, not to be outdone in generosity, later added the neighbouring living of Deane.

George Austen settled at Steventon in 1764, accompanied by a newly acquired wife, Cassandra, daughter of the Reverend Thomas Leigh, Fellow of All Souls College, Oxford. Her connections were more illustrious than her husband's. Her grandfather was brother-in-law to a duke and she had some aristocratic cousins, the Leighs of Stoneleigh Abbey, Warwickshire. Intellectually too she was well-connected; as well as her father being a Fellow of All Souls, her Uncle Theophilus was President of Trinity College, Oxford. He was a well-known character in his day, noted for his sarcastic tongue and a passion for making puns; he even made one on his deathbed. They are not very amusing puns, to judge by the examples that have come down to us, but they seem to have pleased his contemporaries who accounted him a great wit.

Mrs George Austen bore the marks of her kinship with these distinguished relatives. She had an aquiline nose which she was proud of as distinctively

Map of Hampshire showing the villages of Steventon, Ashe and Deane

aristocratic and she much enjoyed jokes. She was herself a humorist – writing entertaining light verses – and a vivacious talker 'uniting,' it was said, 'strong common sense with a lively imagination' and a gift for crisp epigrammatic phrase. There was no question, however, of her aspiring to a wider and more brilliant mode of living. After one of her rare visits to London, 'It is a sad place,' she said, 'I would not live in it on any account; one has no time to do one's duty to God or man.' Born and bred a country woman and by nature contented, she threw herself into the duties of the rural and domestic existence in which fate had placed her. It did not bother her that she was forced to arrive for the first time at her new home sitting alone with many of her belongings on a feather bed perched on top of a wagon; the track leading to Steventon Rectory was too rough going for any more genteel conveyance; and from that day on, her small slight determined figure, dressed usually during these first years in a scarlet riding habit, was always on the go, seeing after children and household and superintending brewing and baking, and cows and chickens.

Cottages at Steventon. Drawing by
Anna Lefroy, Jane Austen's niece

Any pride she may have felt in her ancestry did not check her from discharging her humbler obligations. She did the family mending in the drawing room and went on doing it, even if interrupted by strangers paying a formal call. Yet she still found time and spirit to talk entertainingly and write lively chatty letters reporting the family news to her friends and relations.

Altogether, everything that we know about the George Austens suggests that they were both exceptional and likable; and in their different ways, appropriate parents for Jane Austen. From her father she could acquire a love of literature and a feeling for style, from her mother a sense of comedy and a power of shrewd realistic judgment; from both the confidence inspired by finding herself the child of happily married parents. The circumstances of their life were such as to confirm their happiness. Perhaps the country round Steventon is a little tame – Mrs Austen found it so at first, coming from the then unspoiled beauties of the Thames valley – but it had its charm at once rural and domestic; the charm of its peaceful sheltered villages and wooded, gently sloping hills carpeted in spring with primrose and anemone, its lanes winding between high hazel hedges that opened now and then to disclose airy Constablesque vistas of sky and distant downland.

Steventon church too, though almost as plain and small as a Nonconformist chapel, has a tranquil charm standing, as it does, on a hill apart from the village and with a green grove of trees visible through its clear windows. Steventon Rectory, to judge by the pictures of it that have come down to us, had a similar charm. It is a square, unpretentious, farmhouse-like building with a trellised porch and sloping roof broken by two attic dormer windows. It looks homelike and welcoming and there is a touch of eighteenth-century style about the placing and design of its windows and door. On one side was a pretty old-fashioned garden backed by a thatched wall and shadowed by elm trees; and behind, a little ornamental shrubbery, furnished here and there with rustic seats, beyond which the ground sloped down to the trees and turf of a meadow which was part of the Rectory property. The living had enough land attached to it for George Austen to go in for some farming. This he did partly for pleasure and partly to increase his income. He also added to it by taking in a few chosen pupils. These ranged from the six-year-old Lord Lymington, son of the great local magnate, the Earl of Portsmouth, to Master Vanderstegven, very good-tempered but, poor fellow, fourteen years old and backward. These two joined the Austen household seven or eight years after their arrival at Steventon. Earlier – some reports say during their actual honeymoon – they also took charge of George Hastings, the motherless three-year-old son of no less a person than Warren Hastings, the uncrowned ruler of British India. He had committed his son to their charge on the recommendation of

George Austen's sister Philadelphia, married to Dr Hancock, an English surgeon working in India and a friend of Hastings. To be a delicate child in the eighteenth century meant early death; George Hastings only survived three years. But the Austens were so affectionately kind to him during his brief lifetime that his father remembered them ever after with gratitude. A connection was established between him and them that was to be of some interest in later years. The Austens were to be strong partisans of Warren Hastings when he came to be tried for misconduct in India; Hastings, on his side, was to be an early and distinguished admirer of *Pride and Prejudice*.

It may seem odd nowadays that a dedicated priest of God should have time for all Mr Austen's unpriestly activities. But an eighteenth-century clergyman was regarded, both by himself and others, less as a dedicated priest than as an ordinary citizen whose profession it was to represent society in its moral and religious aspects in the same way as a lawyer represented it in its legal aspects. This meant that, if like George Austen, he was conscientious, conducting the Sunday services regularly, christening, marrying and burying his parishioners when required and also keeping a benevolent and paternal eye on their doings in general. These obligations satisfied, his life was much like that of any other respectable country gentleman. He dressed the same, kept the same kind of company and had plenty of time to occupy himself with whatever interests – scholarly, antiquarian, agricultural – his taste dictated.

And his purse permitted; the clergy in those days were divided into the poor and the better off. George Austen was one of the better off. What with his farm, his pupils and his two livings, he was in possession of a reasonably comfortable income. On the strength of this, he added on several rooms and a bow window to his house and improved its drive and grounds, so that it came to be reckoned much superior to the average run of country parsonages. He also bought a carriage and a pair of horses – these last were also for use on the farm – and, both as host and guest, gratified his and Mrs Austen's taste for social life. This meant the social life of the English country gentry, to be distinguished from that of the nobility on the one hand and, on the other, from that of the commercial and professional classes, with the exception of bankers and barristers. Critics, ignorant of social history, sometimes speak of Jane Austen as coming from the middle class and as such lumped together with George Eliot and Dickens. In fact their families would not have been on visiting terms with Jane Austen's. For she was a child of the gentry, a member of an hereditary ruling class of England, whereas they were not. There was no such gulf between the gentry and the aristocracy. These two together made up the ruling class; and some of the gentry, like Mrs Austen, were related to the aristocracy by blood. They were made further akin by the fact that most of them were landowners or related to those who were. All this made their outlook and manners alike and unlike those of their less privileged compatriots. They cultivated the same pleasures, used the same phrases and, when they did happen to meet, conversed on equal terms and in the same tone. The tone of Jane Austen's own letters is strikingly like that of the clever aristocratic lady letter-writers of her time, Miss Emily Eden or Harriet, Lady Granville: assured, amused, sharply observant of social nuance, and expressing itself in the same crisp ironic language. It is a tone wholly different from that of contemporary middle-class clever women. Jane Austen would have been at home with Lady Granville as she would not have been with Mary Lamb or Dorothy Wordsworth. What kept gentry and aristocracy apart was not class but sometimes politics – the nobles were often Whig, the country gentry generally Tory – and, still more, income. Fabulously wealthy with a great house in London and also several in the country, attended wherever they went by retinues of servants and secretaries and general hangers-on, the eighteenth-century aristocracy lived on a scale and in a style that made continuous and common life between them and the gentry impossible. The Steventon district had its great nobles, Lord Portsmouth of Hurstbourne, Lord Bolton of Hackwood, Lord Dorchester of Greywell, who were on sufficiently equal terms with their humbler gentry neighbours to invite them to a big ball or a garden fête once or twice in the year. But they did not expect to be invited back, and at other times they did not mix with them. County society might rise to include an occasional baronet – Sir Thomas Bertram or Sir John Middleton – but no higher. At the other end of the scale it could admit – given that his manners were gentlemanlike enough – someone like Mr Weston in *Emma*, who had made money in trade but had now set up as a landowner. In general however it was made up of squires and parsons and their families to whom, from time to time, were added visitors in the shape of relations in the army or navy or who worked as bankers or barristers in London.

Well-connected, well-mannered and traditionally Tory, the Austens were qualified in every respect to be welcomed into the inner circle of this society; and all the more because Thomas Knight, chief landowner of the district, lived in Kent, leaving George Austen as his representative to be consulted and deferred to as an acting squire. This did not involve them in any wild whirl of social activities but rather a steady leisurely spaced-out round of morning calls, dinner parties and card parties, varied now and again by some amateur music-making or an expedition to see a local beauty spot or a gathering at a neighbour's garden to eat strawberries or cherries as the season suggested. The gentlemen too – though not so far as we know George Austen – had much

Foxhunting,
by Samuel Howitt

sporting life together, invited each other to shoot, met one another out hunting with the Vyne Pack. Meanwhile young people went in for a good deal of dancing, either once a month in the winter at balls held in the Basingstoke Assembly Rooms or, more informally, in their own homes to the strains of the pianoforte played by one of the older ladies.

There is nothing very unusual in these activities nor in the persons engaged in them. Both seem typical of English county society at any time in the last two hundred years. As such, they might be thought dull. Jane Austen has sometimes been pitied for living in a dull world. Needlessly pitied surely! No doubt there were dull people in it; there are dull people in all societies; the human race is largely made up of dull people. It is likely that the society around Steventon presented, in this respect, a typical cross-section of the human race. Certainly it had its thick-headed ignoramuses: 'Can you answer that which has been troubling me and my wife,' asked a neighbouring squire of George Austen, 'is France in Paris or is Paris in France?' On the other hand, such evidence as we possess suggests that the Austens' immediate circle was far from dull. Not only are Jane Austen's own letters often as clever and en-tertaining as we would expect them to be, but their tone implies that the people she is writing to are amusing and perceptive enough to appreciate them. Further, though her novels do not tell us about her, they do tell us a great deal about the world she lived in; enough to show us that, at its best, it was worthy of her. The conversation at Netherfield, when Elizabeth Bennet was staying there, or at Mansfield Park, when Henry Crawford is trying to win Fanny's heart, portrays a society unusually sharp-witted, cultivated, humorous, articulate and with an easy practised skill in the art of conversation. What girls in fiction are more accomplished talkers than Elizabeth Bennet or Mary Crawford? What man as good company as Mr Bennet or Henry Tilney? These four were, of course, exceptional, but not in such a way as to be at odds with the world they lived in. On the contrary their charm and wit were of the kind that their world would particularly have appreciated. My impression is that the Austens and their close friends were a very favourable example of the agreeability of their age and country, alive with its characteristic blend of style and sparkle and good sense. They never had the chance to be in the company of Dr Johnson or to spend an evening at Holland House, and no doubt if they had they would have been shy and silent: but, if they could have overcome their shyness, they had the qualifications to have got on well in both.

Indeed, for all that, it was distant from the capital, their world was not provincial in the sense that it was out of tune with the great world. On the contrary it was the same world in its rural aspect, rooted in the same cultural and moral traditions and with the same scale of values. Jane Austen makes her judgments with the breadth of view and easy authority of a born and bred woman of the world of her time.

Dancing. Contemporary engraving

II

The range of the Austens' social activities was limited by distance. It extended no further than could be covered by carriage and horse. This was far enough to include various families and their homes. The Chutes of The Vyne, the Mildmays of Dangerfield, the Heathcotes of Hursley, the Holders of Laverstoke, the Terrys of Dummer, the Bramstons of Oakley Hall, the Portals of Freefolk, the Lefroys of Ashe, the Biggs of Manydown, the Digweeds of Steventon, the Harwoods of Deane – these are the names of which we read, as meeting to dine or dance or play cards or follow the hunt in each other's company. One or two names occur more often than others: the Digweeds because they rented Steventon's grey Tudor manor house – they and their curious name seem also to be a popular subject of the Austens' family jokes – the Biggs and Lefroys because they became special friends. But, more frequent than names of friends and neighbours are those of relations. By far the most important family to the Austens was their own.

In those days the term 'family' extended to include many persons: aunts, uncles, first cousins, second cousins, to whom were often added members of the families which these various people had married into. The conscientious biographer grows dizzy as he tries to remember so many different names and to disentangle their connection with the subject of his book. His task is further complicated by the fact that people, especially women, died much younger than now, so that their widowed husband or wife generally married again, thus bringing yet another group of relations into the story. They also produced a new family of children which confused the generation level. Aunts sometimes turn out to be as young as their nieces and stepsons the same age as their stepmothers. The Austens and their connections added to the confusion by calling so many of their children by the same names, very often odd names. We find at least three Cassandras and two Philadelphias in two generations besides strings of Johns and Edwards and Janes and Marys. The Austens' sense of the blood tie was very strong and they kept up in some degree with most of their numerous connections. Even if they did not meet for years on end, they wrote letters to each other and their visits, when they did occur, generally lasted for several weeks.

With some of these relations they became more intimate; among George Austen's relations, Thomas Knight, who had presented him with his living, and also the two Philadelphias: Philadelphia Hancock and her daughter Eliza, and Philadelphia Walter, nicknamed Phila, not a blood relation but a connection of George's mother. The close friends among Mrs Austen's relatives were her brother and sister-in-law Mr and Mrs James Leigh Perrot – James

The Vyne, home of the Chutes who were neighbours of the Austen family

had altered his name because his wife, Miss Perrot, was an heiress – and two clerical families, that of her sister Jane, married to the Reverend Edward Cooper, and that of her cousin Cassandra, wife of the Reverend Samuel Cooke, rector of Little Bookham. All these formed an inner circle of relatives, with whom the Austens regularly exchanged letters and visits. The connections continued into the next generation so that the Austen children grew up in a world peopled by aunts and uncles and cousins and second cousins, most of whom they knew well and some they were very fond of.

There were eight Austen children: James born 1765, Edward born 1767, Henry born 1771, Cassandra born 1773, Francis born 1774, Jane born 1775, Charles born 1779. Another son, George, born 1766, does not come into the story; he was mentally defective and from an early age spent his life away from home. The others, according to the custom of the time, were at first put out to nurse at neighbouring cottages, but, even then, their parents saw them daily and they soon returned home where their parents saw them continuously. George Austen educated his sons himself along with his other

pupils. This meant that James and Henry stayed at Steventon till they were old enough to go to Oxford, while the two youngest, Francis and Charles, remained there till twelve years old, when they went off to Portsmouth to join the navy. The fortunes of Edward, the second son, were different. Mr and Mrs Thomas Knight, the son and daughter-in-law of George Austen's patron, a childless couple, took a fancy to him as a boy. They had him to stay for longer and longer visits till his father began to be worried. Edward, he said, was getting shockingly behindhand with his Latin grammar; should he not be more at home? Mrs Austen did not agree; she had a shrewder sense of priorities. 'I think,' she said, 'you had better oblige your cousins and let the child go.' Since Edward was not a particularly promising Latin scholar, George Austen let himself be persuaded. Edward began to spend more and more time each year with the Knights; in due course of time, Thomas Knight adopted him and made him his heir, the fortunate and future owner of two fine country houses and a great deal of money. The story is evidence of Mrs Austen's realistic good sense. She was rewarded by the fact that Edward remained extremely fond of her – as much so as if they had not been separated.

Edward Austen being presented by his father
to Mr and Mrs Thomas Knight who adopted him

Laverstoke House, home of the Holder family
who lived near Steventon

The Austen daughters, too, spent most of their childhood and youth at home under the care of their parents. This was lucky for them, as it was lucky for their brothers. George Austen was fond of all his children and so was Mrs Austen. They enjoyed their company, took pains with their education, interested themselves in their careers, delighted in their successes. These were frequent. To judge by results, the Austens brought up their children extremely well.

The endpaper of Jane Austen's copy of Fable Choisies

Both in style and substance, it was an eighteenth-century type of upbringing. This is apparent in the letter written by George Austen to his son Francis who was about about to go to sea as an officer, at the age of fourteen.

December 1788

My Dear Francis – While you were at the Royal Academy the opportunities of writing to you were so frequent that I gave you my opinion and advice as occasion arose, and it was sufficient to do so; but now you are going from us for so long a time, and to such a distance, that neither you can consult me or I reply but at long intervals. I think it is necessary therefore, before your departure, to give my sentiments on such general subjects as I conceive of the greatest importance to you, and must leave your conduct in particular cases to be directed by your own good sense and natural judgment of what is right . . .

He begins by gravely reminding him of his religious duties and goes on:

> Your behaviour, as a member of society, to the individuals around you may be also of great importance to your future well-being, and certainly will to your present happiness and comfort. You may either by a contemptuous, unkind and selfish manner create disgust and dislike; or by affability, good humour and compliance, become the object of esteem and affection; which of these very opposite paths 'tis your interest to pursue I need not say.
>
> The little world, of which you are going to become an inhabitant, will occasionally have it in their power to contribute no little share to your pleasure or pain; to conciliate therefore their goodwill, by every honourable method, will be the part of a prudent man. Your commander and officers will be most likely to become your friends by a respectful behaviour to themselves, and by an active and ready obedience to orders. Good humour, an inclination to oblige and the carefully avoiding every appearance of selfishness, will infallibly secure you the regards of your own mess and of all your equals. With your inferiors perhaps you will have but little intercourse, but when it does occur there is a sort of kindness they have a claim on you for, and which, you may believe me, will not be thrown away on them. Your conduct, as it respects yourself, chiefly comprehends sobriety and prudence. The former you know the importance of to your health, your morals and your fortune. I shall therefore say nothing more to enforce the observance of it. I thank God you have not at present the least disposition to deviate from it. Prudence extends to a variety of objects. There is never any action of your life in which it will not be your interest to consider what she directs! She will teach you the proper disposal of your time and the careful management of your money – two very important trusts for which you are accountable. She will teach you that the best chance of rising in life is to make yourself as useful as possible, by carefully studying everything that relates to your profession, and distinguishing yourself from those of your own rank by a superior proficiency in nautical acquirements.
>
> As you have hitherto, my dear Francis, been extremely fortunate in making friends, I trust your future conduct will confirm their good opinion of you; and I have the more confidence in this expectation because the high character you acquired at the Academy for propriety of behaviour and diligence in your studies, when you were so much younger and had so much less experience, seems to promise that riper years and more knowledge of the world will strengthen your naturally good disposition. That this may be the case I sincerely pray, as you will readily believe when you are assured that your good mother, brothers, sisters and myself will all exult in your reputation and rejoice in your happiness . . .

Keep an exact account of all the money you receive or spend, lend none but where you are sure of an early repayment, and on no account whatever be persuaded to risk it by gaming.

I have nothing to add but my blessing and best prayers for your health and prosperity, and to beg you would never forget you have not upon earth a more disinterested and warm friend than,

Your truly affectionate father,
Geo. Austen.

The style is thoroughly eighteenth-century, formal and ceremonious: there is clearly no question of father and son treating one another with any unseemly familiarity. On the other hand, George Austen does address his son on intellectually equal terms, more as if Francis were twenty-four rather than fourteen. The letter is also much of its period in its emphasis on the importance of prudence and politeness and in its judicious mixture of worldly and unworldly wisdom: George Austen is careful to point out that virtue is likely to help you in this world, as well as in the next.

Mrs Austen also blended realism and good principles in her advice to her children. She was too shrewd not to recognize her children's limitations: James, she notes on one occasion, had literary taste and 'power of eloquent composition' but he was not a man of business, whereas Edward was one – though he had not pretensions to James's cultured attainments. However, she adds, 'both are equally good, amiable and sweet-tempered'; and she spoke just as warmly about their brothers and sisters. The children returned their parents' fondness.

III

Indeed home life at Steventon was affectionate, cheerful, untroubled. The actual mode of living was not luxurious. Though comfortably off by country clergymen's standards, George Austen could not afford luxuries. Like its exterior, the inside of the Rectory was plain. Even the drawing room had plain walls, uncrowned by any cornice and with the white painted beams that held up the roof unconcealed by a ceiling. It was sparsely furnished too, with a table, some chairs – presumably well-designed, for this was the eighteenth century, but certainly straight-backed and hard to sit on – and an uncushioned sofa and, by way of decoration, a glass-fronted cupboard containing a gilt china tea service and on the walls a tall pier-glass. The family lived in a way that harmonized with its setting. None of the children had rooms of their own; Cassandra and Jane shared a small one, even after they had grown up. Sons too

Steventon Rectory

brushed their own coats and saw to the grooming of their own horses. Before going out hunting they snatched some breakfast in the kitchen in the glimmering dawn light of a winter morning. None of these things however should be taken as signs of poverty. In those days even dukes' grown up daughters sometimes shared a bedroom and richer young men than the Austens brushed their own coats. Nor did their parents suffer from money worries. The Austen children grew up able to enter fully into any pleasure offered them by county society. They did so wholeheartedly. The boys shot and hunted – they were all enthusiastic sportsmen – the girls embroidered and sketched and played the piano and gossiped agreeably with their neighbours; while both boys and girls danced and dined out and took part in amateur theatricals. Indeed their taste revealed them as very much like the other young ladies and gentlemen who lived near Steventon.

Except in one important particular – they were much cleverer. Home had fostered their cleverness especially on its literary side. They had inherited this from their father and he had encouraged it, partly by reading aloud to them – reading aloud was a great feature of Austen family life – and partly by giving them the run of his library. There they grew acquainted with Pope's poems and Shakespeare's, with the essays of Addison and Johnson, with the novels of Richardson and Sterne and Fielding and Fanny Burney; and all this well enough for references to them and quotations from them to become part of the texture of their conversation. From reading it was a short step to writing;

several of the Austens went in for writing if only skits and occasional verses. They also amused themselves with word games and paper games; and with conversation. Their talk, one gathers, was lively and lighthearted in tone, more concerned with personalities than with ideas or public affairs. What is rare in clever families, it was uncontroversial: 'It was not their habit to dispute or argue with each other, even about small matters,' said an observer.

This was partly because they had been taught to think it very important to keep social life pleasant. It came even more from the fact that they generally agreed with each other. They looked alike, with fine dark eyes, firm mouths and clear cut regular features; several had inherited their mother's aquiline and aristocratic nose. They also tended to think and feel alike. Nature and upbringing had combined to weld them into a corporate personality, actuated by the same principles, biased by the same prejudices, laughing at the same jokes. Prejudices were on the conservative side and disposed them to be cheerfully opposed to anything that struck them as far-fetched or newfangled. The principles were those of the moral and religious orthodox Anglicanism instilled into them by their father; they set a special value on the virtues of unselfishness and self-control, prudence and good humour. When young, this more serious side of them was less in evidence than their jokes. The sense of comedy flourished at Steventon Rectory, exuberant, mischievous, delighting in human absurdity, detecting and making fun of any kind of affectation or silliness or false sentiment. It helped to draw them ever closer together and, with their unusual cleverness, to separate them from other people. It is unlikely that many of the Hampshire gentry laughed at the world as much or as intelligently as did the Austens. Though they liked social life, it meant much less to them than family life. The brothers and sisters were always each other's greatest friends, the people they enjoyed talking to the most. Also those who they loved the best; they were a devoted family. Not however a de-monstrative one; their attitude to life had the limitations of its virtues. Their horror of sentimentality, and perhaps too powerful a sense of the ridiculous, inhibited them from freely and easily expressing deep or tender feeling – even their fondness for each other. When they tried to do so, the result is curiously formal and impersonal. The Austen corporate personality combined qualities not often found together. It was at once affectionate and unsentimental, satirical and good-tempered, orthodox and highly intelligent.

IV

Within the framework of common characteristics, variations showed them-selves. Difference of sex accounts for some of these. The sons took naturally to male pleasures and pursuits, the daughters to female ones. This did not however create any important gulf between them. Sons and daughters alike were cultivated and humorous and sociable. Nor was there any question of one sex looking down on the other. In particular, the sons respected their sisters' judgment and delighted in their wit. The brother and sister relationship played a great part in Austen family life; so also did the relationship between brother and brother and sister and sister. 'Children of the same family,' Jane Austen was to write, 'with the same associations and habits have means of communication which no subsequent connection can supply.' She was talking about William and Fanny Price, but she had drawn these conclusions from her own relation to her brothers.

The members of the family also differed from each other individually. James, the eldest, like his father became a clergyman and was literary. While at Oxford he started and edited a lively periodical called *The Loiterer* and composed poetry about the beauties of nature in the then 'modern' manner of Cowper. In keeping with this, he suffered from occasional moods of melancholy and restlessness and seems to have been a touch more temperamental than the rest of his family. Only a touch though; James was a conscientious clergyman, an excellent family man, made many of the family jokes and wrote comic verses as well as serious. Nor did a Cowper-like love of animals prevent his taking an un-Cowper-like pleasure in field sports. He much enjoyed a day's hunting and, when a young curate, kept a pack of harriers.

Edward, heir to Thomas Knight, had not the same intellectual pretensions; and his portrait suggests that he was less good-looking than his brothers. But he was not dull, had a good head for business and an acute sense of fun. This, combined with a genial indulgent temper, was to make him a popular figure, especially with young people. Next to him came Henry, more complex and, by Austen standards, less satisfactory. As a youth he appeared the most promising of the lot, the handsomest – he had inherited his father's brilliant hazel eyes – the best talker, possessed of the greatest intellectual facility and an infectious gaiety which made him the life and soul of a party. Alas, these agreeable qualities were balanced by weaknesses. His intellectual facility was deceptive. Like his brother James, he went in for writing: but such of it as is left to us is surprisingly undistinguished. He had a mercurial changeable temperament which disinclined him to stick to any course·of life for long and an incurable hopefulness which led him always to think his next move was bound to be successful. 'His hopefulness of temperament,' wrote one of his nieces, 'in adjusting itself to all circumstances, even the adverse, seemed to create a perpetual sunshine.' This remark is double-edged: circumstances can arise for which sunshine is not the appropriate lighting. During the course of

Henry's life he was to be in turn soldier, banker and clergyman. He tired of soldiering, failed as a banker, and, though an eloquent preacher, made no great name for himself in the church. However, he always managed soon to get over failure and disappointment. So did his family. They basked in the sunshine of his cheerful optimism and laughed uncontrollably at his jokes.

There was no question of the last pair of brothers being failures. It is natural to consider them as a pair: both went into the navy and both were unusually able, energetic and reliable, with the result that both were steadily successful. Otherwise their personalities contrasted. Francis, the elder, sounds as if he had been the more forceful. We get a few glimpses of him as a child: a friendly unruly little boy, thrusting his curly head hopefully round the door of a room which he had been turned out of for being troublesome. Nothing ever seemed to frighten him, so his sisters remember, except the sudden bray of a donkey; and, when still of an age to be in the nursery, he started hunting regularly. Precociously enterprising, at the age of seven he bought a pony for £1. 8s. and, after hunting it spiritedly for two seasons in a scarlet coat adapted from his mother's famous riding habit, sold it for £2. 4s. 6d. When he was twelve, he left home for the Royal Naval College at Portsmouth; within three or four years he was in the thick of the Napoleonic War at sea. The navy of the time was a tough and brutal place, but Francis had the spirit to stand up to it. As he grew older, his unruliness disappeared and his energy and enterprise directed themselves on to his profession. By the age of eighteen he had matured into a

(far left) The Reverend James Austen (1765–1819), Jane Austen's eldest brother

(left) Henry Thomas Austen (1771–1850), Jane Austen's fourth brother

(right) Admiral Sir Francis Austen (1774–1865), Jane Austen's fifth brother

short, slight young man, with a soft voice and gentlemanly manners, but formidably firm, independent and efficient; known as a disciplinarian, with a meticulous eye for detail and an unsleeping interest in correct fact which never deserted him, even during a life-and-death crisis. Once, sitting on board ship at anchor, he noticed that a brother officer, swimming in the sea, was being pursued by a shark. 'Mr Pakenham,' cried Francis Austen, 'you are in danger of a shark – a shark of the blue species'; and he thought a chronometer shockingly unreliable because, after five years, it had begun to run five minutes slow! This concern for detail makes his letters rather dull reading, with their lengthy precise recordings of the facts of his voyages and campaigns. But from time to time a well-phrased sardonic sentence reveals their author's Austen blood; as when he speaks of Napoleon 'ennobled to Imperial Dignity by the unanimous suffrages of himself and his creatures', or, after a voyage to the Far East, refers to an encounter with some Chinese mandarins 'which designation perhaps comprises every bad quality which has disgraced human nature'. His literary judgments too have the family humour and perceptiveness. Finally, his religious upbringing had struck a deep root in him. He never swore, even when severely rebuking the men under him – this must have been startlingly rare in Nelson's navy – and he was once remarked on as the only officer who knelt in church: officers in those days usually stood during prayers, with heads bent respectfully down. Back on leave, Francis Austen hated to be idle and occupied himself making bookshelves and fishing nets and children's toys and curtain fringes, all showing delicate manual skill, as well as his characteristic care for detail.

Charles Austen was also religious but sunnier and more boyish. 'Our particular little brother', as his sisters called him when a child, grew up into a handsome lively naval officer, all set to do well and get on and with an impetuous charm of manner which helped him effectively to do so. Popular at sea and at home, he would come home laden with presents for the family and with a robust appetite for parties and dancing. At sea he wrote home letters composed in a pleasant natural style which were passed round the family to the general enjoyment. Both he and Francis kept up steadily with their relations so that, though they were sometimes away for several years on end, the bond between them and their family remained extraordinarily strong. On their side, the family helped to maintain it: the sisters especially interested themselves enthusiastically in their brothers' careers, knew the names of their various ships and fellow officers, loved to hear about the places they visited, rejoiced in any successes they achieved in the way of promotion and prize money. This affectionate interest combined with a vigorous patriotism to make Jane, so little romantic in general, romantic about the British navy.

Captain Charles Austen
(1779–1852), the youngest
son of The Reverend
George Austen

Probably Cassandra was too; history does not tell us. Since few of her letters survive, we know less about her than about her brothers. This is frustrating because she knew Jane more intimately than anyone else and was, throughout Jane's life, the person closest to her. The little we do know reveals her as possessing most of the regular Austen characteristics: their aquiline good looks and their intelligence and piety and family feeling, rather less high spirits than some of the others and rather more of their reserve and undemonstrativeness. Perhaps she had less charm than Henry or Charles; she is praised for 'her judgment and self-command' rather than for any more immediately winning qualities. Moreover she had a reputation for seldom praising anyone and her few letters contain sentences which, taken out of context, sound a little severe and elder-sisterly; as when she says of her brother Edward's children: 'I hope these young people will not have so much happiness in their youth as to unfit them for the rubs that they may meet with afterwards: but with so indulgent a father and so liberal a style of living I am aware that there must be some danger of it.' But we know that she was fond of these particular children and they of her and it is likely that this sentence was uttered in a smiling affectionate tone that did not communicate itself on to the paper. For she could smile; and make others smile too. 'You certainly are the finest comic writer of the present age,' exclaimed Jane in answer to a letter from her. It cannot be said that such writings of Cassandra as have come down to us are noticeably comic, and no doubt Jane was exaggerating in a moment of affectionate enthusiasm. All the same, anything she said on such a subject is certain to have had something in it. If Jane Austen said her sister was amusing, she must have been. For the rest, Cassandra read and sewed and drew portrait sketches good enough to be admired by her friends and relations. When she grew older, she took an interest in the poor of the parish, made garments for them, visited those in trouble and taught some of the village children to read.

2
Early Years

Jane, the second Austen daughter, appeared to follow the family pattern; in looks and tastes and feelings and outlook. She also was lively and reserved and good-looking and good-humoured. In one important respect, however, she did differ from her brothers and sister. She was born an artist, a being endowed by nature with the instinct and capacity to express her creative impulse and her sense of life in the form of a work of art, in her case the art of literature. A number of people are born with something of this impulse and capacity; they are the lesser and part-time artists. A few have both in very intense degree, so that for them it is the centre of existence, the single means by which their nature can fulfil itself. These are the great artists: and anyone aspiring to paint a true likeness of one of them should make his or her relation to their art the main feature of his picture. Jane Austen was a great artist and her relation to her art should be the main feature of any portrait of her. Alas, it is here that her would-be biographer finds himself most frustrated; here it is that he suffers most cruelly from lack of information. Now and again, in her letters, Jane Austen lets fall a brief sentence revealing a shrewd understanding of the technique of novel writing and of the scope and limitations of her particular talent. But neither she nor anyone else ever tells us anything about what her art meant to her or how the fact that she was an artist coloured her view of life. For his view of these things, the biographer has to rely on a few scattered hints and his own guesses.

During her early years he has especially little to help him. Little Jenny – as she was nicknamed during her early childhood – fitted naturally enough into her home. Almost from the start Cassandra, the only other girl in the family, was her chief companion. As her elder – there were two years between them – she assumed a leading and directing role in the relationship. Jane did not mind this. On the contrary she accepted Cassandra's right to a superior position, looked up to her and loved her. She was as affectionate as the rest of her family and as good-tempered. More naturally good-tempered than Cassandra, it seems; for it was said later that Cassandra had the merit of having her temper always under command but Jane had the happiness of a temper that never needed to be commanded. Children are not born self-controlled, they have to learn to be. It is likely that, as a child, Cassandra lost her temper more often than Jane did.

The years passed; it became time for the girls to have some education. George Austen felt himself less qualified to teach daughters than sons, so in 1783 he sent Cassandra and Jane, at the early ages of nine and seven, to Oxford to be educated by a Mrs Cawley, the widow of a principal of Brasenose College. Like so many characters in the Austen story, she was a family connection, the sister-in-law of Mrs Austen's sister, Mrs Cooper, whose daughter, Jane Cooper, was at the same time committed to Mrs Cawley's charge. The experiment was not a success with any of the children. Mrs Cawley was stiff and formal and they did not take to her: for the first time a slight shadow falls across this hitherto sunshiny history. It grew darker, when after a few months Mrs Cawley, for some unrecorded reason, moved to Southampton. Here Cassandra and Jane were suddenly struck down by a dangerous putrid fever. Mrs Cawley decided not to let their parents know about this – she was apparently irresponsible as well as stiff – but Jane Cooper did let them know. Down came Mrs Austen and Mrs Cooper and took their daughters home. Misfortune followed them there. Jane Austen was so ill that she nearly died; while her aunt, poor Mrs Cooper, caught the disease and did die.

The next year, 1784, the Austen parents tried again. This time they sent their daughters to a school near Reading run by a Mrs Latournelle and called the Abbey School because it was partly built out of the ruins of a medieval monastery. Mr and Mrs Austen thought Jane too young to be likely to get much out of the instruction there; but they also realized that to separate her from Cassandra would cause her acute suffering. 'If Cassandra was going to have her head cut off,' said Mrs Austen, 'Jane would insist on sharing her fate.' So they sent Jane too. As a matter of fact, the instruction at Reading does not seem to have amounted to much. Mrs Latournelle, a stout motherly woman with an artificial leg made of cork, was not herself academic: though she had been married to a Frenchman, she had never managed to learn French. More-over, in her view, it was more important for girls to be happy than learned. Unimpeded by her cork leg, she busied herself with organizing excellent meals for them and seeing that their clothes were properly washed and mended. The teaching was left to tutors engaged for the purpose. These did not work their pupils very hard; there were only two or three hours of lessons each morning. The girls spent the rest of their time gossiping and gazing out

The Abbey School, Reading, housed in the gateway to the Abbey

of the traceried windows of the picturesque old rooms or, when it was fine enough outdoors, relaxing in the shade of the tall trees in the spacious garden. Mrs Latournelle did not go in for strict supervision. When some young men, in the shape of Edward Austen, Edward Cooper and a few of their friends, came over to visit their little sisters they easily got permission to take them out to dinner at a neighbouring inn. All this was more enjoyable than life at Oxford with Mrs Cawley, but it was hardly more educational. Perhaps for this reason, after a year Mr and Mrs Austen took their daughters back to Steventon.

They remained there for good. The rest of Jane's childhood and youth was spent at home. It was there, during the next ten years or so, that her character and outlook and tastes gradually developed and took shape. This was not a painful process. Fortunate in having a congenial home, Jane Austen was lucky in having an easy childhood and adolescence. She is one of the few persons of genius who, so far as we know, managed to reach the age of eighteen without having felt noticeably lonely or rebellious or misunderstood. On the contrary, she and her immediate relations understood each other particularly well; and to each other's mutual satisfaction. Jane Austen was fond of all her family. Certain members of it however meant more to her than others. Cassandra much the most; Jane's childish devotion to her had not weakened, rather was it strengthened and confirmed. There was much to unite them. They were two sisters in a large family of brothers and they saw much more of each other than of anyone else. Not only did they share the same bedroom but they spent most of their days together in a little room opening out of it, which served as their own private sitting room. Like the rest of the house, it was furnished sparsely and simply, with an inexpensive carpet patterned with flowers on a chocolate ground, a painted chest of drawers surmounted by a bookcase, an oval mirror hanging between the two windows, a little writing desk with a sloping lid, Cassandra's drawing materials and a piano for Jane. For, while Cassandra was mildly artistic, Jane was mildly musical.

Living together so continuously made them peculiarly intimate and, as a result, frank in a way they could not be with others. All the more because there was between them a natural affinity of spirit: they enjoyed the same pleasures, laughed at the same jokes, agreed in their opinions, respected each other's judgments. Especially did Jane respect Cassandra's. She was always to do so and with a touch of a younger sister's deference. Even after she had made a name for herself as an author, she would insist to her younger relations that Cassandra was wiser and better worth talking to than herself. Cassandra returned her affection with equal strength. Their relationship to each other was to be the most important in Jane's life.

With none of her brothers was she intimate to this degree: but for two, Henry and Charles, she did have a specially soft spot. Henry amused her the most – this was always a very important consideration for Jane – 'he cannot help being amusing,' she once said. Charles appealed to her by reason of his fresh eager charm, all the more compelling when combined with the gallant role of a naval officer. Jane Austen was not at all like Fanny Price; but to Charles, back flushed with boyish triumph from scenes of danger and glory at sea, she responded as Fanny did to her brother William.

II

Indeed Steventon Rectory was the right place to foster Jane's power of affection. It was also the right place to cultivate her taste and educate her mind. Not that either she or Cassandra got much regular teaching there. Presumably, like the Bennet sisters in *Pride and Prejudice*, they could, if they wanted, get special lessons for individual subjects – it can hardly be imagined that Jane taught herself the piano – but, for the rest, they were left to educate themselves by their own efforts. In consequence, Jane, in later life, was to declare herself shockingly uneducated: 'I think I can boast myself,' she wrote, 'with all possible vanity the most unlearned and uninformed being that ever dared to be an authoress.' This remark shows a misleading modesty. She grew up well read in the English classics, prose and poetry, with a reasonable knowledge of history and French, some acquaintance with Italian and, above all, able to express herself in her own language with ease, accuracy and polish. One of the things her nephews and nieces remembered about Aunt Jane and Aunt Cassandra was how admirably articulate they were, how their most spontaneous and casual sentences somehow contrived to be grammatical!

In fact, whatever Jane might say, she had a very good kind of education; that which comes from living with clever people and particularly from the company of a clever father. George Austen must be accounted the person principally responsible for Jane Austen's education. This was partly effected by his practice of reading aloud to his family. It is a measure of the high standard of culture current in the Austen circle that so much reading aloud went on there. At this period it was looked on as an art, involving the careful cultivation of correct tone and diction and expression. George Austen was an accomplished master of this art, an admirable reader alike of novels and plays and poems, including some of the masterpieces of English literature. Jane learned a great deal just from listening to him. She also learned from him in private. After his death she used to speak with emotion of 'his indescribable tenderness as a father' and 'his sweet benevolent smile'. I cannot but believe that he smiled with a special sweetness on his second daughter. If he had such a fine literary taste as people said, he must have perceived something of her unique quality and especially enjoyed talking to her on literary subjects. It was he who woke her feeling for language and style so that she appreciated them in the work of others and cultivated them in her own. This is the most valuable service that anyone can render to a future author. George Austen too could show Jane how to find her way about the five hundred volumes of his library so as to pick out the books most likely to appeal to her.

Two subjects appealed most: literature and history. History, indeed, she read in no very serious spirit. She left behind her a volume of Goldsmith's *History of England* with its margins scribbled over with comments by the twelve-year-old Jane, comments so high-spiritedly partisan as to require capital letters for their adequate expression. Like many girls of her age, though unlike the mature Jane Austen, she is all for the picturesque and the romantic. In particular she is violently pro-Stuart; in her words, a family 'always ill-used, BETRAYED AND NEGLECTED' and 'Oh! Oh! the Wretches!' she exclaims when alluding to those dreadful Cromwellians who opposed them. She is hardly less severe on the Whig Party and its leader Sir Robert Walpole. When for once he is reported to have said something she did agree with, 'spoken like a Tory!' she comments provocatively; and she thought it very wrong of the

Whig government to have made the Highlanders give up wearing kilts. 'I do not like this,' she remarks, 'every ancient custom ought to be sacred, unless it is prejudicial to Happiness.'

Her literary reading was more extensive and her literary judgments much more characteristic. By the time she was in her teens, she had read most of what were always to be her favourite books; and her taste was pretty well fixed. The books she knew best and enjoyed most were contemporary or near contemporary. Like most creative artists, she turned instinctively to those authors who dealt with subjects and in a similar strain to those which stimulated her own imaginative impulse. For Jane Austen this meant realistic accounts of domestic and social life in her own or recent times and especially when treated in a spirit of comedy. Much of the best eighteenth-century literature was of this kind and it therefore interested and influenced Jane Austen as no other literature could, however great. 'No doubt,' says Edmund Bertram in *Mansfield Park*, 'one is familiar with Shakespeare in a degree from one's earliest years . . . to know him in bits and scraps is common enough.' His creator might well have echoed this; living, as she did, under the same roof as George Austen and his sons James and Henry, she cannot have failed to pick up some familiarity with Shakespeare. But there was no question of her knowing him as she knew the great eighteenth-century writers: Addison and Johnson, Sheridan and Goldsmith, Richardson and Fielding and Sterne and Fanny Burney.

It is a mark of the difference between eighteenth-century and Victorian ideas of what was proper that a respectable clergyman like George Austen should have thought it quite all right for his little daughter to read *Tristram Shandy* and *Tom Jones*. As a matter of fact, the mature Jane Austen, though amused by Fielding, did condemn him as morally lax. But this was not Victorian of her, Dr Johnson thought the same. In fact, Fielding and writers like him did benefit her by making her better acquainted than Victorian girls were to be with the tough male world. The result is that, though she never wrote about this world, she does take men more naturally and see them more objectively than most later female novelists were able to do, neither shrinking nervously from their masculinity nor vainly trying to imitate it. As a matter of fact, Fielding's unillusioned perception of human weakness and the robust but well-bred irony with which he expressed it should have appealed to her, for her own had something in common with it. Yet she learned more from Richardson and Fanny Burney; from Fanny Burney's specifically feminine line in social comedy and from Richardson's psychological insight. His novels enthralled her like no others. She read and re-read *Sir Charles Grandison* till she knew it almost by heart. It became part of the permanent furniture of her

Part of Jane Austen's manuscript of
a play, entitled Sir Charles Grandison or The Happy Man,
A Comedy, *adapted from* The History of Sir Charles
Grandison *by Samuel Richardson*

mind: and later she was to dramatise episodes from it, presumably for family performance.

These are the novelists Jane Austen took seriously. But, like all novel addicts, she also enjoyed those which she did not have to take seriously. Luckily she lived in an age that provided them. Two types were readily available: novels of Sentiment, designed to stimulate agreeable tears, and novels of Terror, designed to awake agreeable shudders. In the novels of Sentiment, the hero and heroine were both persons of extreme sensibility, usually throughout the book divided by scruples of extreme delicacy. Their stories were diversified by love scenes, rapturous or pathetic, by death scenes, swift or lingering but always poignant, and involving outpourings of feeling – amorous, conjugal, parental, filial – all equally intense and refined. The novels of Terror, set in some vague but picturesque foreign country and in some vague but picturesque historic period, told of haunted castles and sinister monks and mysterious crimes and high-born villains intent on the ruin of high-born beautiful maidens. Both kinds of book found their way into Steventon Rectory to be devoured delightedly by the Austens in general and by Jane in particular. She was pleased to find them absurd as well as absorbing. This mixed reaction was later to prove an inspiration to her own work.

She read poetry as well as prose; here her brother James was her guide and preceptor. Ten years older than her and down from Oxford for vacation, he took an elder brother's pleasure in influencing and directing his little sister's taste. Once again it was a taste for contemporary authors; in particular Cowper, whose first works appeared in the 1780s. They were marked by qualities likely to appeal to her: a delicate sense of the domestic scene, a demure humour and, above all, a power of depicting the English landscape in its gentler aspects. Jane Austen took great pleasure in natural beauty – 'The beauties of nature must for me be one of the joys of Heaven,' she was later to say. It was a straightforward kind of pleasure. There was no Wordsworthian mysticism about it, no sense of nature as the visible manifestation of a divine spirit; and, while she preferred landscape to look natural, her feeling was less for the wild and the grand than a steady quiet enjoyment of the friendly countryside she knew, with its woods and streams and fields and hedgerows. For her its familiarity was part of its charm; it meant that it was enhanced by all manner of personal memories and associations. Strong patriot that she was, she liked it better for being English. It is characteristic that she ends her account in *Emma* of the pretty view to be obtained from Mr Knightley's grounds by remarking, 'It was a sweet view – sweet to the eye and the mind, English verdure, English culture, English comfort seen under a sun bright without being oppressive.'

Dr Samuel Johnson, by James Barry

*(opposite) William Cowper,
by G. Romney, 1792*

Another favourite writer was Johnson. Her feeling for him was different from that she felt for the poets and novelists; and more significant. 'My dear Dr Johnson' so she spoke of him. She did not speak like that of any of them; for whereas she thought of them primarily as artists, she thought of Johnson primarily as a man, and one profoundly sympathetic to her. His brilliance and his oddness were both of a kind that especially amused her. More important, he voiced, and with unique force, the point of view of the society to which she belonged and of whom the Austens were outstandingly representative; with its characteristic blend of hard-headed good sense and traditional culture and Anglican piety.

The piety is especially to be noted. Jane Austen's religion, so her biographer discovers as he studies her, is an element in her life of the highest significance and importance. The Austen reticence kept her from ever talking much about it. But the little she did say, and what her intimates said about her, show that she grew up to be deeply religious. She actively practised her faith and her moral views were wholly, if unobtrusively, determined by the dictates of the Christian religion as interpreted by her church. The seeds of her faith were sown early and at home by her father's teaching; it was developed and strengthened by private devotions and by the services she went to at the little Steventon church.

She did not, however, always find it necessary to be serious in church. George Austen used to employ her to help him to make up the entries in the parish registry; among them, those noting weddings. Specimen pages were provided to show the prospective brides and bridegrooms where to fill in their names. Jane, by way of brightening these, would sometimes fill in her own

name as the specimen bride of a specimen bridegroom, an imaginary figure
with a name invented by her. These entries are still to be seen in the registry:
on one occasion, she calls the bridegroom Edmund Arthur William Mortimer
of Liverpool, on another, and less gloriously, Jack Smith, apparently a
homeless vagabond, for he is given no place of residence. George Austen
allowed these entries to remain on the register. Clearly he did not object to
some mild fun in church.

III

Indeed, during Jane Austen's youth and until well after she had grown up,
there was plenty of fun to be had at Steventon. Life there continued untroubled. The passing of time brought changes: James and Henry grew up
and left to spend the terms at the family college of St John's at Oxford;
later, though at the younger age of twelve, Francis and Charles went off in

St John's College, Oxford

turn to join the Royal Naval Academy at Portsmouth. Meanwhile Edward, in order to acquire the knowledge of the world suitable to the heir to a fortune, was dispatched by Mr and Mrs Knight on a Grand Tour of Europe. But sailors and Oxonians alike came regularly home on leave or on vacation; and Edward spent time there too. All of them took an active part in what they later remembered as 'a life made pleasant by the flow of native wit with all the fun and nonsense of a large and clever family'. It was a social life with parties in the neighbourhood and frequent visitors to give pleasant variety to life at home. The visitors most often mentioned were relations, notably the Coopers and the Leigh Perrots. The Coopers lived part of the year at Bath and the Austen girls used to stay with them there. Also with their rich Uncle and Aunt Leigh Perrot: these divided their time between their Bath residence and a country house called Scarlets in Berkshire. Mr Leigh Perrot sounds the more likable of the two: kindly, cultivated and like his sister, Mrs Austen, an amusing talker. His wife was less popular, a hard-featured formidable woman with a capricious temper and a powerful will, which, as an heiress, she was accustomed to exercise unopposed. But she had her merits; had a strong sense of family duty and was a good wife to her husband who loved her and, as her future history was to show, had the strength of character to stand up against misfortune. She appreciated the Austen sisters and was good to them. Jane's visits to her and to the Coopers at Bath contributed to her education as a novelist, for they gave her her first chance to observe human nature as it displayed itself in town life and with all the added variety of character and differing social milieux that town life affords.

Her acquaintance with these things was also enriched by the visits to Steventon of two other relations, her Aunt Philadelphia Hancock and, still more, her aunt's daughter Eliza. Most of Jane's relations are dim and faceless figures today; we know too little about them for this to be otherwise. But out of the general dimness one more individual face does emerge, the small, piquant, black-eyed countenance of Eliza Hancock. Jane had known her for as long as she could remember. Dr Tysoe Hancock had brought his wife and daughter to England from India in 1765. In 1769 he went back to earn some more money; a few years later he died there. Meanwhile Philadelphia and Eliza remained in England, spending a great deal of time at Steventon. Long enough to become very much part of the family: George Austen came to feel an affectionate responsibility for his niece. After her husband's death, however, Philadelphia Hancock, for reasons unrecorded, went off to live abroad, settling finally in Paris. There Eliza grew up, sociable, vivacious, attractive

Philadelphia Hancock,
Jane Austen's aunt

enough to gain an entrance into fashionable Parisian society and, if we are to trust her own account, to become a success there. In 1781, at the age of twenty and actuated by prudence rather than passion, she married a French officer, Jean Capotte, Comte de Feuillide. It was during his courtship that Eliza first introduces herself to posterity in a series of letters written over the next twelve years to a girl of her own age and an English connection, Philadelphia Walter.

Eliza de Feuillide, daughter of Philadelphia Hancock

The letters are a comical and disarming mixture. In tones of innocent self-satisfaction and with an evident desire to dazzle and impress her less fashionably placed correspondent, she intersperses detailed descriptions of new fashions in clothes and hair styles and rapturous accounts of elegant fêtes and court balls at Versailles with sentimental professions of affection and solemn expressions of gratitude to heaven for having provided her with so enviable a social position and so loving a husband. 'He literally adores me,' she writes, 'entirely devoted to me and making my inclinations the guide to all his actions.' Her inclinations did not always guide her to stay at his side; nor, after a time, does this seem to have distressed him. For, when in 1786 Eliza found herself with child, she and her mother, encouraged by Monsieur de Feuillide, left for England to remain there till the child was born. Eliza spent her stay partly in London, where she managed to be received at the English Court, partly at Bath and a great deal at Steventon. George Austen had been much upset by her marriage to a foreigner and a Roman Catholic; but now she was back, as lively as ever, still safely a Protestant and able to regale the company at the Rectory with sparkling accounts of the fashionable gaieties of Paris and descriptions of Queen Marie-Antoinette, resplendent in diamonds and transparent silver gauze and adorned 'with an amazing large bouquet of white lilac'.

There are hints too of Eliza embarking on a mild flirtation with Henry Austen. With his hair powdered and dressed 'in a very townish style', he showed her round the Oxford colleges. She longed to be a Fellow, she said, so delighted was she by the black gown and becoming black cap. Nor was this flirtation too mild to be enlivened by some agreeable tiffs and reconciliations. Handsome, erratic Henry Austen was, as might be expected, the most flirtatious of the Austen brothers and often entangled with some attractive young woman or other. The Christmas of 1787 saw Eliza at Steventon, with her baby safely born, and herself ready to play a part in some private theatricals. They were far from being the first theatricals to take place there. The Austens were keen amateur actors, and sometimes produced two plays in a year; in the summer in a barn, which they fitted out as a theatre, in winter in the Rectory dining room. These productions were carefully planned and organized affairs, for which James Austen generally wrote an appropriate prologue and epilogue. He wrote one this time to introduce two comedies in both of which Eliza de Feuillide played a leading role. She wanted Philadelphia Walter to take part too, but Philadelphia refused on the grounds that she felt shy; she would prefer, she said, to come as a spectator. This would not do at all, replied Eliza reprovingly; Mrs Austen had said she had no room in her house at such a time for 'idle young persons'. The tone of Eliza's letters and that of Philadelphia's answers give the impression that, while still protesting undying affection, they no longer cared much for one another – perhaps they never had! Eliza's incessant harping on her brilliant social life had nourished in Philadelphia a growing and envious irritation, which now found vent in censoriousness. She had lately been staying with Eliza at Bath and had now come to the conclusion, so she told her brother, that, though not without some good qualities, Eliza was indefensibly thoughtless and her way of life dangerously frivolous.

If so, it was not going to be so for long. Eliza's next few years were to be marked by a succession of misfortunes. In 1789 the French Revolution broke out, signifying the end of the regime on which the de Feuillides' whole mode of living rested; and, all the more fatally, because Monsieur de Feuillide was a fervent royalist. After a sojourn in France, Eliza and her son came back to England to stay with her mother. In 1792 her mother died. Philadelphia Walter – she emerges from the correspondence as singularly unlovable – could not conceal some satisfaction that Eliza was at last reaping the just consequences of her pleasure-loving past.

> Poor Eliza [she wrote to her brother] must be left at last friendless and alone. The gay and dissipated life she has long had so plentiful a share of has not ensured her friends among the worthy: on the contrary many, who otherwise have regarded her, have blamed her conduct and will now resign her acquaintance. I always felt concerned and pitied her thoughtlessness. I have frequently looked forward to the approaching awful period, and regretted the manner of her life, and the mistaken results of my poor aunt's intended, well-meant kindness: she will soon feel the loss and her want of domestic knowledge. I have just wrote to assure her she may command my services.

History does not relate whether Eliza accepted this last offer; if made in this tone, it seems unlikely. Meanwhile the 'awful period' of her life continued. 1793 saw the start in France of the Reign of Terror. A year later Monsieur de Feuillide was arrested in Paris and guillotined as an Enemy of the Republic.

Eliza's story strikes a startlingly incongruous note in an account of Jane Austen's world. But it had its place there; for it shows that this world was not so cut off from the sensational melodrama of contemporary history as her novels were to suggest. Jane Austen may have had no personal experience of court balls or bloody revolutions, any more than she had of the naval battles in which her brothers were later to be engaged, but she did hear all these things talked about by people who had been themselves actually involved in them. The reason why there is nothing about them in her novels is that they did not provide the kind of material that stimulated her creative powers; and she had the self knowledge to realize this. The private theatricals in which Eliza took part at Steventon did provide her with the right kind of material. She was to make memorable use of it, over twenty years later, in *Mansfield Park*.

She also found much to stimulate her interest and curiosity in the lives and characters of her friends. Cassandra and she had a number of these; girls of their own age and rank living in the neighbourhood. Their greatest friends came from two families in particular. Elizabeth, Catherine and Alethea Bigg, along with their brother Harris, lived at the home of their parents Mr and Mrs Bigg-Wither, Manydown Park near Basingstoke. There was a good deal of coming and going between Manydown and Steventon: when the Austen sisters were old enough to go to dance at the Basingstoke Assembly Rooms, they used to spend the night at Manydown. Greater friends still were Mary and Martha Lloyd. They entered the Austens' life in 1788 when their father became rector of the neighbouring parish of Deane. Mrs Lloyd was the daughter of a Lady Craven, famous in her day for being very beautiful and very wicked. Her daughter and granddaughters were neither, but they were sensible and civilized and there was some special affinity of spirit between them and the two Miss Austens. In consequence of this, acquaintance blossomed quickly into close friendship. The Reverend Mr Lloyd died in 1789; three years later, his widow and daughters moved a little further off to

Deane Church. Drawing by Anna Lefroy

the village of Ibthorpe. But they and the Austens managed to keep up with each other: the link between the two families was not weakened. With Martha Lloyd, who enjoyed the same kind of jokes as Jane and Cassandra, it became strengthened. For the rest of their lives she was to be their most intimate friend.

In these early years however, she is a less important character in Jane Austen's history than an older friend. This was Mrs Lefroy, wife of the Reverend Isaac Lefroy, Rector of Ashe, living in a spacious elegant house a few miles from Steventon. She was known in the district as Madam Lefroy; the designation suggests that she was recognized as deserving to be distinguished from the ordinary run of commonplace people. Madam Lefroy was a personality, gifted and considerable enough to be thought worthy of two columns of high-flown obituary in the *Gentlemen's Magazine* after her death. She made her first impression on the world very early, writing a much-admired hymn at the age of twelve, to be followed a few years later by some poems published in the *Poetic Register*. Later and after marrying the Reverend Mr Lefroy, she turned her attention to philanthropy, throwing herself into welfare work among the poor children of the neighbourhood, teaching them to read and write and make baskets and even – for she was a pioneer in health matters – vaccinating eight hundred of them with her own hands. This did not prevent her from finding time for other activities. Now and again she dashed off a copy of verses aglow, it was said, 'like her conversation, with careless forcible rapidity'. She also made her house a social centre where old and young met to dine and dance and talk. Animated, enthusiastic and with a winning manner, she was an admirable hostess and must have had an unusually perceptive eye for quality in others; for she was the first person of whom we have record to notice that there was something special about Jane Austen. She had her often to her house, sympathized with her, encouraged her and drew her out. To be singled out for special notice by an attractive older man or woman is a great event in an intelligent young person's life. Jane Austen felt it to be so and responded to Madam Lefroy's kindness with an enthusiasm equal to hers; she enjoyed her conversation, appreciated her charm and her looks, especially what she was later to describe as 'her eager look of love'. With the passing of years, the relationship was to settle into a steady friendship and one a little different in kind from any other we hear of in Jane Austen's life. To her, Madam Lefroy was always to shine out as a figure still irradiated by the ardent glow of her youthful grateful admiration.

Madam Lefroy had a brother, Egerton Brydges, who met the young Jane Austen several times at Ashe Rectory in the late 1780s. In old age he recorded his remembered impression of her. 'My eyes told me,' he wrote, 'that she was fair and handsome, slight and delicate but with cheeks a little too full.' He also said that he never suspected that she was an author.

IV

This is hardly to be surprised at for Jane Austen was at most fifteen years old at the time. But in fact, though unremarked outside her own family, her genius had already begun to bestir itself; so actively that, well before she was in her teens, she was spending a large part of her time in writing. She used to say in later days that she wished she had not: she would have done better to have spent her time educating herself by reading. I cannot think she was right about this. No amount of extra reading could have made the novels she was to write any better; and posterity would have been the poorer for the loss of her youthful productions. She herself must have been pleased with them: for, years later, to amuse her relations she collected and copied out in three volumes a selection from what she had written between the ages of eleven and eighteen. They are slender little volumes and their contents trifling enough, consisting mainly of squibs and skits on the light literature of the day: comedies, popular histories, sentimental novels. As their author grew older, the pieces, while remaining exclusively comic, became less extravagant and more realistic; enough to include some satirical sketches of character. The last item – she must have been fully eighteen by the time she wrote it – is an unfinished short novel called *Catherine*, an essay in what was to be her characteristic vein of high comedy. Slight as they are, these early writings are of the highest interest to anyone trying to get to know Jane Austen. For in them, and for the first time, we hear her voice.

It is recognizably her voice. Here is a quotation from a very early burlesque: 'In Lady Williams every virtue met. She was a widow with a handsome jointure and the remains of a very handsome face.' Or again:

> 'Miss Dickins was an excellent Governess. She instructed me in the Paths of Virtue; under her tuition I daily became more amiable, and might perhaps by this time have nearly obtained perfection, had not my worthy Preceptoress been torn from my arms, e'er I had attained my seventeenth year. I never shall forget her last words. "My dear Kitty" she said "Good night t'ye." "I never saw her afterwards" continued Lady Williams wiping her eyes, "She eloped with the Butler the same night."'

These are unmistakenly by the author of *Northanger Abbey*: here at the age of thirteen she strikes the authentic Jane Austen note. This means a comic note.

Her early works demonstrate that Jane Austen's was primarily and basically a comic genius: her original literary impulse was an impulse to make her reader laugh. This was always to remain an integral part of her inspiration. Some critics – literary critics are for the most part a solemn race – forget this. They discuss her work with an unsmiling seriousness more appropriate to those of Dostoyevsky or D. H. Lawrence. Of course, Jane Austen's masterpieces do reveal a profound insight into man's moral nature and, as such, are, in the best sense of the word, extremely serious. But they are none the less comic for that. Man is such an odd animal, such a mixed untidy bundle of follies and inconsistencies and incongruities, that it is impossible for a discerning observer to look at him for long without smiling. Certainly Jane Austen could not; with the result that to the end of her life and in her most penetrating studies of men and women she hardly writes a paragraph unlit by the glint of a smile. In these, her first efforts, she is smiling all the time or, rather, she is uproariously laughing. But already her amusement is of a piece with that of her maturity, that is to say stirred largely by the spectacle of affectation and silliness and sentimentality. She writes too in the same demurely mischievous tone. Her youth added zest to her mischief. Though precocious in her power of expression, she was very much a girl of her age in what she found laughable. She was a normal robust-minded child – and living in the robust-minded eighteenth century, she was allowed to show it – who much enjoyed jokes about supposedly solemn and shocking subjects. The plots of her skits in-volved drunkenness and childbirth and illegitimate children and deaths of all kinds, including murder and suicide; and their author gets a great deal of fun out of them all. But it is a characteristically Jane Austen kind of fun; there is nothing heavy-handed or 'sick' about it, only an impish infectious gaiety. Listen to the sensitive romantic-minded Laura describing the deathbed of her sensitive and romantic-minded friend Sophia:

> Her disorder turned to a galloping Consumption and in a few Days carried her off. Amidst all my Lamentations for her (and violent you may suppose they were) I yet received some consolation in the reflection of my having paid every Attention to her, that could be offered, in her illness. I had wept over her every Day – had bathed her sweet face with my tears and had pressed her fair Hands continually in mine –. 'My beloved Laura (said she to me a few Hours before she died) take warning from my unhappy End and avoid the imprudent conduct which has occasioned it . . . Beware of fainting-fits . . . Though at the time they may be refreshing and agreeable yet believe me they will in the end, if too often repeated and at improper seasons, prove destructive to your Con-stitution . . . My fate will teach you this . . . I die a Martyr to my grief for the

loss of Augustus . . . One fatal swoon has cost me my Life. Beware of swoons
Dear Laura . . . A frenzy fit is not one quarter so pernicious; it is an exercise to
the Body and if not too violent, is I dare say conducive to Health in its
consequences – Run mad as often as you chuse; but do not faint –.'

These were the last words she ever addressed to me . . . It was her dieing
Advice to her afflicted Laura, who has ever most faithfully adhered to it.

Equally entertaining, equally characteristic, is the burlesque, spiritedly
illustrated by Cassandra, that she wrote on a popular history of England.
Irreverently she comments on the learned Lady Jane Grey and her Greek
studies:

Whether she really understood that language or whether such a study proceeded only from an excess of vanity, for which I believe she was always rather
remarkable, is uncertain. Whatever might be the cause, she preserved the same
appearance of knowledge and contempt of what was generally esteemed
pleasure, during the whole of her life; for she declared herself displeased with
being appointed Queen; and, while conducted to the scaffold, she wrote a
sentence in Latin; and another in Greek, on seeing the dead body of her Husband
accidentally passing that way . . .

This history shows also that Jane Austen's youthful romantic feelings were
never so strong as to extinguish her sense of comedy. On the contrary they
become an occasion for it: she even enjoys making fun of her own enthusiasm
for the Stuart family, and her arch-heroine, Mary Queen of Scots:

Oh! what must this bewitching Princess, whose only friend was then the Duke
of Norfolk, and whose only ones now Mr Whitaker, Mrs Lefroy, Mrs Knight
and myself, who was abandoned by her son, confined by her Cousin, abused,
reproached and vilified by all, what must not her most noble mind have suffered
when informed that Elizabeth had given orders for her Death . . .

From the very start, Jane Austen was an ironist; and just as ready to be ironic
about herself as about other people.

From an early age too, she showed a formidably keen eye to perceive
human folly. Her later sketches and the unfinished story of *Catherine* are
evidence that she watched the people she encountered at Steventon and Bath;
and noted their absurdities to very good purpose. Clearly she has met elderly
ladies like Mrs Stanley: '"Queen Elizabeth," said Mrs Stanley, who never

hazarded a remark on history that was not well founded, "lived to a good old age and was a very clever woman"'; or silly girls like Camilla:

> All her stock of knowledge was exhausted in a very few Days, and when Kitty had learnt from her, how large their house in Town was, when the fashionable Amusements began, who were the celebrated Beauties and who the best Milliner, Camilla had nothing further to teach, except the Characters of any of her Acquaintance, as they occurred in Conversation; which was done with equal Ease and Brevity, by saying that the person was either the sweetest Creature in the world, and one of whom she was dotingly fond, or horrid, shocking and not fit to be seen.

The mature Jane Austen could not have pin-pointed the weaknesses of Camilla or Mrs Stanley more sharply than this; and she would have done it in just the same tone of voice, with the same mixture of the cheerful and the merciless. Jane Austen was always to delight in her fools: without compunction she mocks their follies so as to get all the amusement out of them she can. But, just because she enjoyed them so much, they do not put her out of temper; rather she recognizes them as an addition to the pleasures of life. This was as true of her at seventeen as at thirty. Even more so; for at seventeen her natural gaiety was increased by the exuberance of youth. The outstanding characteristic of these early works is their rollicking high spirits. From these alone we could deduce that the young Jane Austen enjoyed her existence.

But only by implication; no more than in her later writing does she talk about herself. Nor did she write just for herself. These pieces were composed also to amuse her family and her friends. Many of them are prefaced by humorous dedications to one or other of them: to Cassandra or Charles, or Jane Cooper or Martha Lloyd. Sometimes the pieces contain a reference to the person addressed: a story mentioning the navy for instance is dedicated to Francis, her sailor brother. Many authors start writing in order to relieve their private feelings; Jane Austen began in order to contribute to family entertainment. Her early works were examples of a family activity and expressions of a family outlook. Her mother wrote comic verses, several of her brothers wrote satirical sketches; and their satire too was often directed against sentimentalism and affectation. Henry Austen, in the Oxford magazine he edited, attacked Sentimental novels as likely to spread 'a degenerate and sickly refinement among their female readers . . . which may lead them to fall martyrs to their own sensibility'. His sister Jane was in no danger of suffering this fate; her account of Sophia's death is a light-hearted variation on the same theme. The outlook expressed in it was the Austen family outlook. More, it was the outlook of the whole society to which they belonged. During the previous thirty or forty years many other English writers had made fun of the Sentimental Movement and from a similar point of view to Jane Austen's.

Yet her ridicule cannot be mistaken for theirs. For hers is still amusing and theirs is not. This is partly because her humour is of a finer and more lasting quality; it is even more because she is better at putting it across. Her touch is lighter and more certain; she writes better. Her crisp deft style seems to have been hers almost from the first moment she put pen to paper. It was not as an original spirit but as an accomplished mistress of her craft that this parson's teenage daughter so easily and obviously surpassed her predecessors.

Altogether these first trifling works do turn out, on investigation, to tell us a great deal about Jane Austen, the artist; about the primary nature of her inspiration, and the history of its development. We learn from them that she was a precocious genius, in her style, in her power of observation, in her characteristic vein of humour. This precocity was encouraged by favourable circumstances. The world she lived in was peaceful, stable and secure; it gave her time and tranquillity to follow her literary bent. Further, though it did not look up to a writer as a superior kind of being, it was not Philistine. On the contrary, it was cultivated and literary. Many of the Austens wrote themselves. For this very reason, though they enjoyed Jane's work, they did not make too much of it, did not encourage her in such a way as to make her self-conscious, or ambitious to attempt tasks beyond her powers. The mental climate in which she grew up enabled her genius to develop unhampered, undistracted, unforced.

3

Steventon Days

So much for Jane Austen the budding author. But what about the Jane Austen who was not an author, Miss Jane Austen the budding young lady? Was she also precocious? Did her personality and demeanour grow to maturity with a similar speed and smoothness? On the little evidence we possess, the answer to this last question seems to be 'not quite'. The authority for this is Jane Austen herself. Writing nearly twenty years later, she praises the easy friendly agreeability of the new generation of children, the fact that they suffer so little from what she calls the 'Moral Disease of Shyness'; and are in this so unlike herself at the same age, 'so that it makes me feel overcome with astonishment and shame'. Shyness may be the explanation of a curious account of her at thirteen years old. It comes in a letter from Philadelphia Walter to her brother; she had met the Austen parents and their two daughters when they were staying with Uncle Francis Austen at Sevenoaks.

> Yesterday I began an acquaintance with my 2 female cousins, Austens. My uncle, aunt, Cassandra & Jane arrived at Mr. F. Austen's the day before. We dined with them there. As it is pure Nature to love ourselves, I may be allowed to give the preference to the Eldest who is generally reckoned a most striking resemblance of me in features, complexion & manners . . . The youngest (Jane) is very like her brother Henry, not at all pretty & very prim, unlike a girl of twelve: but it is hasty judgement which you will scold me for. My aunt has lost several fore-teeth which makes her look old: my uncle is quite white-haired, but looks vastly well: all in high spirits & disposed to be pleased with each other . . . Yesterday they all spent the day with us, & the more I see of Cassandra the more I admire [her] – Jane is whimsical & affected.

One need not be blindly biased in Jane's favour to find this harsh picture unconvincing. The skits and burlesques she was writing during this very year make it clear that she was the reverse of prim and that she had a ruthlessly sharp eye for affectation in others and a delight in laughing at it. It is unlikely that she herself should have been prim or affected. Shyness however can make people self-conscious; and self-consciousness can give the effect of affectation. It can also make people appear stiff and therefore prim. Philadelphia goes on to criticize Jane for being 'whimsical', a term which, in those days, signified given to opinions so odd and indefensible as only to be taken as the expression of irrational personal whims. For the intolerant Philadelphia, this would have meant opinions she happened to disagree with. It is very possible that Jane's views were different from Philadelphia's. This is hardly to her discredit: Philadelphia's letters to Eliza de Feuillide show her to have been silly and prejudiced. Jane Austen would quickly have discovered this, nor was she of an age to conceal her discovery: she was too young to have acquired the art of tactful insincerity. Philadelphia, realizing this, would have taken a dislike to her: hence her hostile description. Her bias is further shown by her saying that Jane was not pretty, for all other descriptions of Jane comment on her good looks. It was in the very same year that Madam Lefroy's brother speaks of her as 'fair and handsome, slight and elegant'.

When she was not writing, Jane Austen's life continued to follow the same pattern as that of other country clergymen's daughters of her rank in life: helping in the house, going for walks, doing needlework, taking an occasional lesson in music or sketching or dancing, amusing herself in the company of her family, friends and neighbours. Years went by; in the course of time she 'came out', that is to say, was judged old enough to be allowed to take part as a grown-up person in grown-up social life: dining out, going to balls, and making the acquaintance of eligible young men. For, so far as girls were concerned, marriage was the serious and ultimate objective of all social life and social pleasures. The age at which a girl came out varied with the views of her parents. Lydia Bennet, we know, came out at fifteen: but her creator indicates that this was rare and too young. The age approved by Mr and Mrs Austen was likely to have been at least a year later. At sixteen then, Miss Jane Austen made her first appearance on the stage of the world as a grown-up young lady. Since she was in essentials the woman she was to remain during the first phase of her mature existence, it seems a suitable moment to pause and take a look at her.

She presents a pleasant spectacle. 'I hear,' wrote Eliza de Feuillide, 'her sister and herself are two of the prettiest girls in England . . . perfect beauties and of course gain hearts by dozens.' This must be taken as an example of Eliza's fashionable gush rather than as a statement of exact truth; no one else ever described either Jane or Cassandra as 'perfect beauties'. But it is clear that both were noticeably pretty girls; and, what was of more importance, pretty in the style admired by the gentlemen of the period. Jane's features, though small and well-formed, were less regular than Cassandra's – as Egerton Brydges had pointed out, her face was too full and round-cheeked – but this was more than compensated for by a more brilliant complexion, a livelier expression and the general effect her personality conveyed of glow and health and animation. She was a brunette with a clear olive skin, dark hair clustering around her face in natural curls, bright hazel eyes like her father's and a tall graceful figure. Grace was one of her outstanding characteristics; it showed in her dancing – she loved dancing – and in the light firm step with which she walked. Another characteristic was neat-handedness. Her handwriting was exquisitely neat, so was the way she folded and sealed her letters – this was before the days of envelopes – so was her needlework. There still exists a tiny beautifully stitched bag she made at the age of seventeen, as a present for Martha Lloyd, containing thread, needles and a minute pocket containing some complimentary verses inscribed in a miniature delicate hand.

> This little bag, I hope, will prove
>   To be not vainly made;
> For should you thread and needles want,
>   It will afford you aid.

> And, as we are about to part,
>   'Twill serve another end:
> For, when you look upon this bag,
>   You'll recollect your friend.

It was not in Jane Austen to be clumsy. She shone at any activity that required the deft use of fingers and hand. Finally, to her other physical attractions she added that of a charming and expressive voice.

These advantages made 'coming out' less of an ordeal for her than it was for some girls. We do not hear any more about her shyness. She had learned to conceal, if not wholly to overcome it: and by the time she grew up, it was sufficiently under control to be no impediment to her enjoying the new pleasures open to her as a fully grown-up young lady. She did enjoy them. Like the other girls of her acquaintance, she liked balls and dinner parties, took a lively though not obsessive interest in dress and fashion; and, as much as other girls, was interested in young men. She was attractive enough to have little trouble in getting on with them. No doubt Eliza de Feuillide was once again indulging in her habit of gushing extravagance when she said that Jane and Cassandra were gaining hearts by dozens. But she could have said nothing of the kind if either of them had been known failures at getting themselves liked by young men. They may not have been heart-breakers, but they were pleasing enough to find no difficulty at getting partners at any ball they went to.

Some writers have even suggested that the young Jane Austen was too enterprising in pursuit of the other sex. This view is grounded on a sentence from the reminiscences of Mary Russell Mitford; she says that her mother, who lived near Steventon, recalled Jane as 'the prettiest, silliest, most affected, husband-hunting butterfly she ever remembered'. On examination these sharp words turn out to have little evidence to support them. For one thing, Mrs Mitford left the Steventon district when Jane was only ten years old, so that she can only be speaking on hearsay. For another, the description – more so even than that by Philadelphia Walter – is at variance with everything else we know about Jane Austen. Whatever false impression she may have made at twelve years old, it is incredible that the grown-up Jane Austen, the Jane Austen who, within a few years, was to create such devastating embodiments of silliness and affectation as Lucy Steele and Isabella Thorpe, should herself have ever appeared as affected, let alone silly. Or husband-hunting; though, like most girls of her age, she probably considered any young man she met in the light of a possible husband. Altogether Mrs Mitford's account must be considered mainly worthless. Personally, I should be sorry to regard it as wholly worthless. I like to think there was a time in Jane Austen's life when she could be called a pretty butterfly. I know of no other woman writer of the first rank who has been similarly described.

II

Indeed Jane Austen seems to have found it easy to lead two independent lives. There was no friction, let alone conflict, between the activities of the author and those of the girl newly launched into the social life of the Hampshire gentry. Though Jane Austen's creative impulse was so strong, it co-existed comfortably enough with any taste she may have had for balls and dinner parties. This was partly because she did not have to go to a great many of these: even at its liveliest, existence at Steventon left plenty of time for writing. It was even more because social activities, so far from hampering her creative impulses, stimulated them. She may have enjoyed them as much as the girls around her did, but her reaction to them was ultimately different from theirs. For them the ultimate interest lay in the possibilities they offered for love and marriage; instinct and education alike had taught them that in these alone could they find fulfilment. Not so Jane Austen. No doubt she could be attracted by young men and must have had occasional thoughts of marriage.

She had no quarrel with the orthodox feminine world she was born into; never complained that it was limited or evinced the slightest wish to break away from it. But ultimately she was detached from it, an artist, a contemplative, absorbedly and amusedly concerned to observe and reflect on its inhabitants as nourishment for what was – whether she was conscious of it or not – the vital principle of her existence. For her the primary interest of social life lay in its power to fertilize her imagination. The people she met in society did not know this; like Egerton Brydges, they never suspected she was an author. To the young men she danced with she was just another girl of marriageable age; more attractive than some, but with no apparent signs of potential genius.

This was lucky for her. No more then than now did most young men feel at home with female geniuses. They did not even like girls to be conspicuously intelligent or well-informed. Jane Austen was soon aware of this, as a quotation from *Northanger Abbey*, an early novel, was to illustrate:

> ... where people wish to attach, they should always be ignorant. To come with a well-informed mind is to come with an inability of administering to the vanity of others, which a sensible person will always wish to avoid. A woman, especially, if she have the misfortune of knowing anything, should conceal it as well as she can. . . . I will only add, in justice to men, that though to the larger and more trifling part of the sex, imbecility in females is a great enhancement of their personal charms, there is a portion of them too reasonable and too well-informed themselves, to desire anything more in a woman than ignorance.

This unillusioned reflection is clearly the fruit of personal experience. Not however an embittering experience; Jane is amused not annoyed by male fatuity. Herself, she had not much suffered from it. She knew enough men, in particular her own father and brothers, who fully appreciated her feminine intelligence.

Her silence about her literary activities involved her in no painful effort of self-control: she preferred it that way. But it did mean that she led a sort of double life: and this had its effect both on herself and on the impression she made on others. Jane Austen's sense of a hidden difference between herself and the people she met in company cannot but have increased her innate reserve and confirmed in her any shyness she may have retained since childhood; with the result that there was always to be a striking difference between Jane Austen at home and as she appeared in company. In company she was one of the two pretty Miss Austens, pleasant, composed and elegant. At home she revealed at least some glimpses of the penetrating, ironic student of the human comedy who was to write her novels. It is a significant fact that, unlike everyone else who had met her, her brothers and sister were not surprised when these novels appeared and made her famous.

Jane Austen was better able to enjoy being grown-up and the pleasures it brought with it because, during the next two years, life at Steventon continued untroubled. From time to time its even tenor was diversified by occasional visits – to Bath and Scarlets and elsewhere – and, more importantly, by family events. But these too were mostly cheerful, consisting, as they did, of weddings; and – what is rarer – weddings equally welcome from the personal and the worldly point of view. The first occurred in December 1791 when Edward married Elizabeth Bridges, the pretty amiable daughter of a rich gentleman of title, Sir Brook Bridges. The couple settled down in a country house near Godmersham called Rowlings, given them by the Knights. Here was another pleasant house for Jane and Cassandra to go and

Elizabeth Austen née *Bridges*
(1771–1808), Edward's wife

stay at. Next year Edward was followed to the altar by his elder brother James, recently ordained and established as curate first at Overton, near Steventon again, but soon to move still nearer to his father's second parish of Deane. James's bride was also a good match: she was the daughter of General and Lady Anne Mathew, the owners of the neighbouring Manor House of Laverstoke. Helped by an allowance from his father-in-law, James was unusually comfortably off for a country curate, able to keep his pack of harriers

The Mathew family: James Austen's first wife was Anne Mathew

and to set up a private carriage for his wife. Finally, in the summer of the same year, Jane Cooper became engaged to Captain Williams of the Royal Navy. Since her father had lately died, shortly before Christmas she was married at Steventon. This marriage turned out a good thing for the Austens. These were the days of patronage in His Majesty's Services and Captain Williams was later able to help advance the career of Charles Austen. Altogether, what with balls and weddings and visits and the presence of personable young naval officers, 1792 was a gay time for the two Miss Austens.

The year 1793 saw the appearance of the first fruits of the two Austen weddings. Edward's wife gave birth to a daughter Fanny and James's to a daughter Anna. Both girls were later to be important figures in their Aunt Jane's life. The year was further brightened by the return home of Francis Austen after two years abroad with the Fleet in the East Indies. He had done well enough to have been made Lieutenant at the early age of seventeen. It was also in this year that Henry Austen gave the first signs of that changeableness which was to render his life story more chequered than that of his brothers. He had gone up to Oxford intending to become a clergyman like James. Now he was taken with a fancy for military life and managed to get himself accepted as a Lieutenant in the Oxfordshire Militia; to become no doubt a magnet of attraction to the many Lydias and Kitty Bennets in the towns where his regiment happened to be stationed.

Nothing important happened to the Austens in 1794. In 1795, however, it was Cassandra's turn to become engaged to be married. Her fiancé, the Reverend Thomas Fowle, was no stranger to the family. He was a connection of the Lloyds through Mrs Lloyd's family, the Cravens, and had also been a pupil of James Austen: there is a mention of him speaking a prologue written by James Austen at one of the family theatrical productions. Personally then, he was a native of the Austen world and one they approved of. The only obstacle to the marriage was lack of money. However, the Earl of Craven, a friend as well as a relation of Thomas Fowle's, promised him the rich living of Ryton, of which he was the patron, when it should fall vacant. This was not likely to be for a year or two; in the meantime Lord Craven, who was a soldier, had orders to go with his regiment to the West Indies. He offered to take Fowle with him as the regimental chaplain while waiting for the vacancy. After some hesitation and discussion, he accepted. Cassandra settled down to wait his return. For some unspecified reason, it was judged more discreet that neither Lord Craven nor anyone else outside the Fowle and Austen families should be told of the engagement.

In the same year and for the first time the young Austens met with calamity. Their life sounds secure compared with our own, but in one respect it was more vulnerable. Medical science was far less advanced and early death was a common occurrence. In May, James's wife Anne suddenly died. Her daughter, Anna, a child of two, wandered round the house of mourning; 'Mama, Mama!' she kept pathetically asking. This was more than her bereaved young father could bear; he sent her off to Steventon to be looked after, for the time being, by her aunts. It was not long before her mother had faded from the child's memory to become no more than a dim figure of a tall slender lady dressed in white; the aunts had come to fill her place. There was no doubt that Anna's favourite of the two was Aunt Jane. She followed her about the house, calling for her to entertain her. Aunt Jane was always glad to respond. She was not sentimental about children: and in *Sense and Sensibility* and *Persuasion* she has described spoiled and tiresome children with such ruthless and entertaining accuracy that some people have concluded she disliked them. In fact, she liked children very much and they liked her. She enjoyed their company, interested herself in their characters, had a turn for devising new games and amusement for them. Above all she excelled in telling them stories, comical, whimsical, fantastic chronicles that sometimes went on in instalments for days on end. Little Anna was the first member of the next generation to benefit by this gift for story-telling.

It was not confined to stories for children. The unfinished tale of *Catherine* had been only the first of several successive efforts at novel writing. Undistracted apparently by births and deaths and weddings and the return from foreign parts of delightful brothers, Jane Austen's literary activities during these years flourished and developed. Already by 1795 she was engaged on preliminary studies for her early masterpieces. By 1796 she had begun to work on *First Impressions*, the earlier version of *Pride and Prejudice*.

III

For her biographer, this year is even more of a landmark. 1796 is the date of her first surviving letters, that in which we get the first instalment of her lifelong correspondence with Cassandra. This means that it gives us our first chance of hearing the voice of Jane Austen the woman, as distinguished from that of Jane Austen the author. It is a less expressive voice: Jane Austen, and especially when writing to Cassandra, is not one of the great letter-writers. She is too unpretentiously concerned just to retail the family news or give useful information, reporting that brother Charles has been promoted or noting that coquelicot is now the most fashionable colour at Bath. Further, the particular traditions of reserve Jane Austen was brought up in tended to inhibit her spontaneity. Her sense of fun bubbles forth easily enough but not her graver, tenderer sentiments, so that her letters lack variety of tone and mood. All the same, those to Cassandra do bring us closer to Jane Austen the woman than we get anywhere else: with no one else was she so candid. Jane Austen later came to have a name among her friends – perhaps she had always had it – for not speaking ill of other people. She was said never to 'quiz' people, that is to say make fun of them by way of being amusing. Her letters confirm this reputation – always excepting her letters to Cassandra. In these she is blithely and formidably outspoken to point out any faults or foibles she may note in others and gaily ready to make outrageous jokes about them; jokes that, more than anything in the novels, reveal her as a child of the high-spirited, unsqueamish eighteenth century. The effect of this has been to scandalize some later readers who, more in sorrow than in anger, have reproached her for making jokes in poor taste. These readers forget the period she lived in and misapprehend the nature of her relation to Cassandra. Any acute observer of his or her fellow men must often be critical of them; and, if he or she happens like Jane Austen to be a humorist, will make fun of them. But if, also like Jane Austen, he or she is discreet and dislikes giving pain, they will reserve their criticism and jokes exclusively for the ears of the few persons who are really in their confidence. For Jane, this meant Cassandra. Only with Cassandra did she let herself be as frank and flippant as she felt inclined, say what she really thought about other people, sure that her remarks would be taken in the spirit in which they were intended and certain that they would not be repeated.

The difference in tone between her letters to Cassandra and to anyone else is proof that with Cassandra she was intimate as with no one else. Intimate but not demonstrative: these letters are sparing of endearments. Even with Cassandra, the Austen habit of reserve persisted. In *Emma*, Jane Austen speaks with strong, if amused, approval of the way that after months of separation George and John Knightley greeted one another 'in the true English style, burying under a calmness that seemed all but indifference, the real attachment which would have led either of them, if requisite, to do anything for the good of the other'. What was true of the Knightley brothers was true of the Austen sisters. Admirably English though it may be, this undemonstrativeness can make the letters to Cassandra sound a little cool. Cassandra of course would not have found them so; she knew what Jane felt about her. But it is important to realize that they are eminently private documents and only to be rightly understood if read as such. Transmitted to the printed page and published, they can give a misleading impression: cool and sometimes trivial. Read in the right context they are not cool at all and no more trivial than are most family letters. Now and again they are very amusing indeed.

This is especially true of the earlier letters written in Jane Austen's cheerful youth. But let her speak for herself: she does it better than I can speak for her. Here are some passages from letters written in January 1796 to Cassandra who was on a visit to her future husband's family near Newbury. Jane gives her the social news of Steventon with especial reference to another nephew of the Lefroys, young Tom Lefroy from Ireland, with whom Jane had been having a flirtation.

> You scold me so much in the nice long letter which I have this morning received from you that I am almost afraid to tell you about how my Irish friend and I behaved. Imagine to yourself everything most profligate and shocking in the

Thomas Langlois Lefroy (1776–1869).
Miniature by Engleheart

way of dancing and sitting down together. I can expose myself, however, only once more, because he leaves the country soon after next Friday, on which day we are to have a dance at Ashe after all. He is a very gentlemanlike, good-looking, pleasant young man, I assure you. But as to our having ever met, except at the three last balls, I cannot say much; for he is so excessively laughed at about me at Ashe, that he is ashamed of coming to Steventon, and ran away when we called on Mrs Lefroy a few days ago.

In the autumn it was Jane's turn to go visiting. She writes to Cassandra from her brother Edward's house, Rowlings.

My Dear Cassandra, I shall be extremely anxious to hear the event of your Ball and shall hope to receive so long and minute an account of every particular that I shall be tired of reading it. Let me know how many besides their fourteen selves and Mr and Mrs Wright, Michael will contrive to place about their Coach, and how many of the Gentlemen, Musicians and Waiters he will have persuaded to come in their shooting jackets . . . We were at a ball on Saturday I assure you. We dined at Godmersham and in the evening danced two country dances and the Boulangeries. Elizabeth played one country dance, Lady Bridges the other, which she made Henry dance with her; and Miss Finch played the Boulangeries – On reading over the last three or four lines I am aware of my having expressed myself in so doubtful a manner that if I did not tell you to the contrary, you might imagine it was Lady Bridges who made Henry dance with her, at the same time that she was playing – which if not impossible must appear a very improbable event to you. . . . Mr Richard Harvey is going to be married; but as it is a great secret and only known to half the neighbourhood, you must not mention it.

Jane had no Tom Lefroy to flirt with at Rowlings; but she seems to have been sufficiently amused there writing and talking to her brothers; Frank too was staying at Rowlings.

Edward and Frank [she writes] went out yesterday very early in a couple of shooting jackets and came home like a couple of bad shots for they killed nothing at all. They are out again today and are not yet returned. Delightful spirit! – they are just come home; Edward with his two brace; Frank with his two and a half. What amiable young men!

These letters surely are very like letters written by Elizabeth Bennet. The plot of *Pride and Prejudice* and the characters and circumstances of the Bennet family were utterly unlike anything in Jane Austen's own story. But for once, even if unintentionally, she did draw her heroine partly from herself.

The flirtation with Tom Lefroy continued to feature in Jane's life for the next year or so. At first it is clear from the tone of her letters that it was a light-hearted affair.

> Tell Mary [she had written in January 1796] that I make over Mr Hartley and all his society to her, for her sole use and benefit in future, and not only him, but all my other admirers into the bargain wherever she can find them, even the kiss which C. Powlett wanted to give me, as I mean to confine myself in future to Mr Tom Lefroy, for whom I don't care sixpence.

And then the day after:

> At length the day has come on which I am to flirt my last with Mr Tom Lefroy, and when you receive this it will be over. My tears flow as I write at the melancholy idea!

In fact the flirtation was not over: it lingered on into 1798 and it seems as if Jane's feelings became a little more serious. Certainly Tom Lefroy's feelings for her did; and openly enough to worry his uncle and aunt, who thought him too young and too poor to think of marriage. To stop this, they immediately packed him off home to Ireland. Jane, it was thought, did suffer a twinge of disappointment, enough to keep her proudly silent when Mrs Lefroy happened to mention Tom's name, but not enough to disturb their friendship. This was just as well, for within a year Tom Lefroy had recovered enough to get engaged to another girl and one who had the advantage over Jane of possessing a considerable fortune. He lived on to become Lord Chief Justice of Ireland. As an old man, he recalled his love for Jane Austen, with a slight sense of guilt at the speed with which he got over it. 'It was a boy's love,' he explained apologetically.

All this is to anticipate. In the meantime 1797 had been marked for the Austens by a number of events. In January, James Austen married again. His bride was Jane and Cassandra's friend Mary Lloyd and they were naturally delighted. Mary Lloyd had a brusque manner and a plain face scarred from smallpox; but they had known her for years and always found her sensible and good-humoured. Jane was especially pleased and Mrs Austen wrote her future daughter-in-law an enthusiastic letter of congratulation.

> Had the selection been mine [it ran] you, my dear Mary, are the person I should have chosen for James's wife, Anna's mother and my daughter. Being as certain

as I can be of anything in this uncertain world, that you will greatly increase and promote the happiness of each of the three.

Mrs Austen spoke too soon: Mary Lloyd turned out less satisfactory as relation than as friend. As Mrs James Austen, she may have promoted her husband's happiness, but she got on badly with her step-daughter Anna and was not over friendly to her mother- and sisters-in-law. Very soon she showed herself displeased if James went often to see them. In later years she was to be the only member of the family of whom Jane was to speak sharply.

Some months later it was Henry's turn to get married. He had for the last year or two become once more sentimentally entangled with his widowed cousin, Eliza de Feuillide, and had even proposed to her. She hesitated and Henry turned his volatile attention to a Miss Pearson, tartly described by Eliza as 'a bright wicked-looking girl with bright black eyes which pierced through and through'. Miss Pearson rejected him; he proposed again to Eliza. This time she agreed to have him. As before, when accepting poor Comte de Feuillide, she was careful to point out that she did so from reason rather than

Portman Square; Upper Berkeley Street, where the Henry Austens lived, can be seen on the left of the picture

Sydney Smith, by H.P. Briggs

passion: also as before, she stated with some satisfaction that her fiancé was so devoted and accommodating that he gave her the pleasure of having her own will in everything. As a matter of fact, Henry Austen seems also to have been able to please himself. After a year or two, during which his profession sometimes took him away for months on end, he left the army and became a banker; the couple settled down to a lively social life in London. In 1801 Philadelphia Walter, irritated by another example of what, in her view, was Eliza's undeserved good luck, reported on them with restrained asperity:

I spent one day with our cousins the Henry Austens. She is much the same, but talks of retiring into Wales and resigning the world, in which he seems perfectly to agree. He has given up the army. They live quite in style in Upper Berkeley Street, Portman Square.

It was in 1797 that Edward Austen reaped the full benefits of being adopted as a son by Mr and Mrs Knight. Thomas Knight died in 1794 leaving to his wife for her life his fortune and Godmersham, the fine eighteenth-century country house where he lived. Now his widow announced that she wanted to surrender the house and most of the money to Edward. For the future, when the Austens went to stay with him, it was at dignified and spacious Godmersham.

The year 1797 however, like 1795, was far from being all weddings and happiness. In February news came from San Domingo in the West Indies that Thomas Fowle, Cassandra's fiancé, had died from yellow fever. The news was made, if possible, harder to bear with resignation when it was learned that Lord Craven had said that he would not have risked taking Fowle with him, if he had known of his engagement. Too much discretion could, it seems, be as dangerous as too little. For Jane, loving Cassandra as she did, Fowle's death was intensely distressing, though her distress was mingled with admiration for the extraordinary self-control and lack of egotism with which Cassandra met her bereavement.

Later in the year, by way of giving them a change, Mrs Austen took her daughters to stay with their relations at Bath. This visit is interesting in that it may have provided Jane with a model for her fiction – and a celebrated one. In the winter of that year, there was staying at Bath a young clergyman called Sydney Smith, tall, pleasant-looking and extraordinarily amusing in a vein of humour peculiarly his own. He was employed by a family called Hicks Beach as tutor to their son; the Hicks Beaches knew the Austens. A year later Jane began to write a novel later to appear as *Northanger Abbey*, in which the heroine visiting Bath meets a tall, pleasant-looking young clergyman called Henry Tilney, extraordinarily amusing and in a vein of humour very like that of Sydney Smith. Can there be any connection between these two events? Nothing, I am afraid, that can be called real evidence, no record that the two ever met – though, many years later, Sydney Smith was to profess himself an admirer of Jane Austen's novels. I fear that, in suggesting a connection, I may be yielding to a temptation that often besets biographers, namely to put forward a view on insufficient grounds just because I should like it to be true. But I cannot resist doing so. Sydney Smith was the most entertaining talker and Jane Austen the most entertaining writer of their time. Moreover their view of life at once unillusioned and good-humoured, robust and ironic, shows a close affinity of spirit. It would be delightful to think that one inspired the other.

Most, if not all, of *Northanger Abbey* in its first version was to be written in 1798. In 1797, Jane Austen was still at work finishing *First Impressions*. Fond as she was of Cassandra and her brothers, their joys and sorrows cannot have been her only or even her main concern during these years: they must have often come second to her writing. For this was her first great creative period, that in which her genius, now pretty well matured, irresistibly poured itself forth. The first versions of *Sense and Sensibility, Pride and Prejudice* and *Northanger Abbey* were all written between 1795 and 1798. No doubt they were none of them as good as the final versions were to be; they are likely to have lacked both the technical accomplishment and the subtler insights that come from greater experience of art and of life. But her previous writings and also her letters make it certain that they were already extremely amusing. Little Anna Austen, who liked her aunts better than her stepmother, still managed to spend a good deal of time at Steventon. In old age she re-membered listening several times at a closed door there and hearing Aunt Jane reading aloud a story to her Aunt Cassandra and both of them going off into fits of laughter at it. She heard the names of some of the characters in the story – can it have been those of Mrs Bennet or Mr Collins? – and talked about them afterwards downstairs. Immediately and earnestly her aunts took her aside and told her that the story was their secret and she must never speak of it again to anyone but them.

Was it also kept a secret from the Reverend George Austen? If so, this was only before it was finished: for then he read it and with great pleasure. He was an admirer of Fanny Burney – a year before he had subscribed to buy her latest novel *Camilla* as a present for Jane – and was delighted that a daughter of his should follow in her footsteps. Accordingly in November 1797, he wrote to a London publisher called Cadell saying he was in possession of the manuscript of a novel, about the length of Fanny Burney's *Evelina*, which he would send to him if he would consider publishing it: he also asked what would be the cost of publishing it at the author's expense; he meant at his own. Cadell wrote back a refusal. As he never saw the book he cannot be severely blamed; but his harsh punishment has been to be remembered, if at all, only as the man who refused to read the book that afterwards turned out to be *Pride and Prejudice*. We do not know how Jane herself reacted to his refusal. But she must surely have been disappointed, even disheartened. She was never to have much confidence in the merit of her books. The manuscript of *First Impressions* was put away; it was some years before she began to work on it again.

IV

In 1798 – none survive from 1797 – the letters begin again. The first, written in the spring, is a letter of condolence written to Philadelphia Walter on the death of her father.

My dear Cousin,

    As Cassandra is at present from home, you must accept from my pen, our sincere Condolence on the Melancholy Event which Mrs Humphries's letter announced to my father this morning. The loss of so kind and affectionate a Parent, must be a very severe affliction to his Children, to yourself more especially, as your constant residence with him has given you so much a more constant and intimate knowledge of his Virtues. But the very circumstances which at present enhance your loss, must gradually reconcile you to it better; the Goodness which made him valuable on Earth, will make him Blessed in Heaven. This consideration must bring comfort to yourself, to my Aunt, and to all his family and friends; and this comfort must be heightened by the considerations of the little Enjoyment he was able to receive from this World for some time past, and of the small degree of pain attending his last hours. I will not press you to write before you would and otherwise feel equal to it, but when you can do it without pain, I hope we shall receive from you as good an account of my Aunt and yourself, as can be expected in these early days of Sorrow. My father and mother join me in every kind wish, and I am my dear Cousin

Your affectionate
Jane Austen.

Apart from the different nature of its subject matter, this letter is noticeably different in manner from those of Jane Austen's that we have seen before. Compared with them, it sounds stilted and impersonal; we do not hear her voice in it. But it is of great help to anyone trying to paint her portrait; for it reveals, as the earlier letters do not, some different and important aspects of her personality. It sets it firmly in its period. It is formal because men and women then believed in formality, especially when speaking about the solemn things of life. They thought that just because death was a momentous event, to talk of it informally would be to talk of it inadequately. A well-brought-up young girl like Jane Austen was taught to express herself in a letter of condolence with appropriate ceremony. Jane Austen's disposition was such as to intensify this formality. Natural shyness combined with the Austen tradition of reserve to make it peculiarly hard for her directly to express serious sentiments: this was later to be a problem for her as an author. When, as here, she had to write a letter of condolence, she tended, out of embarrassment, to express herself stiffly and formally, even judged by the standards of her period.

Luckily for her reputation as a letter-writer, the occasion for letters of condolence did not happen often. Life at Steventon remained in general untroubled and, in the other letters we have from her during the next year or two, we find ourselves back with the lively youthful Jane Austen who reminds us of Elizabeth Bennet. They are written when either she or Cassandra is away on a visit. Since these visits often lasted as long as two months, the main purpose of the letters was to keep Cassandra up with the news about family and friends and fashions and balls and dancing partners, together with the gossip of the neighbourhood. Family news comes first; Mr Austen is reading Cowper's poems aloud to his wife and daughter and, to himself, a new novel of Terror called *The Midnight Bell*; Mrs Austen's liver is out of order, also her chest – with advancing years she had become something of an invalid. Jane writes much about her brothers; especially she retails any scrap of news about the two away at sea, tells that Charles wants to transfer to a frigate, exclaims with enthusiastic joy on learning that Frank has been promoted to be a Commander. There are also the brothers at home to talk about: James and his unsatisfactory wife, admirable Edward – 'I know of no-one more deserving of happiness unalloyed' – and his children; in particular the three-year-old George, 'Itty Dordy' as he called himself, who had taken a flattering fancy to his Aunt Jane.

> My dear Itty Dordy's remembrance of me is very pleasing to me – foolishly pleasing, because I know it will be over so soon. My attachment to him will be more durable. I shall think with tenderness and delight on his beautiful and smiling countenance and interesting manners, till a few years have turned him into an ungovernable ungracious fellow.

These remarks are characteristic. Unsentimental Jane Austen, even in her most affectionate moments, remains unillusioned and humorous.

Indeed the spirit of comedy dances over this early correspondence; it is at its most exuberant and mischievous when Jane is out to entertain Cassandra with the latest gossip of the neighbourhood. Here again, we are back in the eighteenth century; this time not the solemn eighteenth century of formal condolences but the robust and sparkling eighteenth century of the wits and humorists. Let examples illustrate:

> Mrs Portman is not much admired in Dorsetshire; the good natured world as usual extolled her beauty so highly that all the neighbourhood have had the pleasure of being disappointed.

Miss Blachford is agreeable enough. I do not want people to be very agreeable, as it saves me the trouble of liking them a good deal.

Mrs Hall of Sherborne was brought to bed yesterday of a dead child some weeks before she expected, owing to a fright. I suppose she happened unawares to look at her husband.

Charles Powlett gave a dance on Thursday to the great disturbance of all his neighbours, of course, who, you know, take a most lively interest in the state of his finances and live in hopes of his being ruined . . . his wife is discovered to be everything the neighbourhood could wish, silly and cross, as well as extravagant.

People get so horribly poor and economical in this part of the world that I have no patience with them – Kent is the only place for happiness – everyone is rich there.

In passages like these, Jane Austen's letters are for once as amusing as her novels.

Indeed her pleasure in the human comedy, together with her good sense, taught her to make the most of any chance of enjoyment that came her way.

Our ball was chiefly made up of the Jervoises and Terrys, the former of whom were apt to be vulgar, the latter to be noisy. I had an odd set of partners: Mr Jenkins, Mr Street, Colonel Jervoise, James Digweed, J. Lyford and Mr Briggs, a friend of the latter. I had a very pleasant evening, however, though you will probably find out that there was no particular reason for it; but I do not think it worth while to wait for enjoyment until there is some real opportunity for it.

Even if she had to content herself with some odd partners, Jane Austen contrived to have a pleasant evening. It is in sentences like these that she reminds us of Sydney Smith; as when he says 'whether one lives or dies I hold and always have held to be of infinitely less moment than is generally supposed; but if life is the choice, then it is commonsense to amuse yourself with the best you can find wherever you happen to be placed.'

In 1798 Jane Austen managed to acquire another admirer. Samuel Blackall, a young Fellow of Emmanuel College, Cambridge, met her in the summer at the Lefroys' and was sufficiently attracted to consider coming back at Christmas-time, in order to get to know her better with a view to possible matrimony. Jane returned his feelings even less than she had returned those of Tom Lefroy. She had nothing to say against his moral character, but she found him all too fond of instructing young women at great length and in a loud voice. This was lucky; for Blackall soon discovered that his prospects were not good enough to allow him to marry yet. He wrote to Mrs Lefroy to tell her so. She showed the letter to Jane, who commented:

> This is rational enough; there is less love and more sense in it than sometimes appears before, and I am well satisfied. It will all go on exceedingly well, and decline away in a very reasonable manner. There seems no likelihood of his coming into Hampshire this Christmas, and it is therefore most probable that our indifference will soon be mutual, unless his regard, which appeared to spring from knowing nothing of me at first, is best supported by never seeing him.

She never saw him again but remembered him well enough to be interested fifteen years later to learn that he was at last engaged to be married to a Miss Lewis.

> I should very much like to know what sort of a woman she is [she commented]; he was a piece of Perfection, Noisy Perfection, himself whom I always recollect with regret . . . . I would wish Miss Lewis to be of a silent turn and rather ignorant, but naturally intelligent and wishing to learn; and fond of cold veal pies, green tea in the afternoon, and a green window blind at night.

Meanwhile the tide of her literary energy went on flowing strongly. It is probable that it was during this period that she wrote the short novel called *Lady Susan*; she certainly started the first version of the book that was ultimately to turn into *Northanger Abbey*. *Lady Susan* is unlike anything else she wrote. For one thing, it is set in a grander milieu, and for another it deals with a more obviously wicked character. The central figure, Lady Susan Vernon, is a sort of blue-blooded Becky Sharp, an unscrupulous adventuress, far more sensational in her evil doing than any character in Jane Austen's later books. It starts with Lady Susan already saddled with a bad reputation; the action describes how she tries to get herself well married and received back into respectability. She also plots to achieve a worldly marriage for her reluctant and virtuous daughter. This daughter in the end is saved for a happier fate, while Lady Susan herself is united to a foolish baronet much younger than herself. The novel has its merits. It is lively and readable all through, and Lady Susan's own letters are unusually entertaining.

All the same, *Lady Susan* is not a success. Jane Austen is working outside her experience. She had no acquaintance with smart society and has to describe it from hearsay; with the result that her picture lacks the intimate reality with which she portrays the country gentry. We may suppose that she recognized this, for she made no effort to have the book published in her lifetime and never again wrote about a world of which she had no personal experience. By trial and error, she was gradually learning her art.

There is no question of *Northanger Abbey* being a failure. Starting as a take-off of the popular novel of Terror and Sentiment rather in the manner of the burlesques of her childhood and written in the same rollicking high spirits, it soon turned into realistic comedy, drawing on her personal memories of life at Bath or in the country. By the time she had finished it, 1798 had turned into 1799, and 1799 into 1800. Life did not alter much while this was happening. As in previous years, its uneventful round was varied by occasional visits to Bath, Godmersham and Ibthorpe, by balls at one or other of the neighbouring country houses or at Basingstoke Assembly Rooms. News came from Frank telling how he had had the honour of personally delivering important dis-patches to Nelson himself in the Mediterranean; Charles came back more than once on leave, out to enjoy himself at the local dances and with his hair cut short in a fashionable 'crop', a mode disapproved of by his conservative-minded brother Edward. Meanwhile Jane's letters to Cassandra continued crisp, cheerful, entertaining. Here are some quotations from them:

> A Doctor Hall is in such deep mourning that either his mother, his wife, or himself must be dead.

> [At Bath] We are exceptionally pleased with the house; the rooms are quite as large as we expected. Mrs Bromley is a fat woman in mourning and a little black kitten runs about the staircase. . . . We have two very nice sized rooms with dirty quilts and everything comfortable.

> Mrs Bramston's little moveable apartment was tolerably filled last night by herself, Mrs H. Blackstone, her two daughters, and me. I do not like the Miss Blackstones; indeed, I was always determined not to like them, so there is the less merit in it. Mrs Bramston was very civil, kind and noisy. I spent a very pleasant evening, chiefly among the Manydown party. There was the same kind of supper as last year, and the same want of chairs. There were more dancers than the room could conveniently hold, which is enough to constitute a good ball at any time.

> Soon after our return to Dean a sudden invitation and our own postchaise took us to Ash Park, to dine tête à tête with Mr Holder, Mr Gauntelett and James Digweed; but our tête à tête was cruelly reduced by the non-attendance of the two latter. We had a very quiet evening, I believe Mary found it dull, but I

thought it very pleasant. To sit in idleness over a good fire in a well-proportioned room is a luxurious sensation. Sometimes we talked and sometimes we were quite silent; I said two or three amusing things, and Mr Holder made a few infamous puns. I have had a most affectionate letter from Buller; I was afraid he would oppress me by his felicity and his love of his wife, but this was not the case; he calls her simply Anna without any angelic embellishments, for which I respect and wish him happy.

Another example of the Austen dislike of too openly demonstrative affection:

It was a pleasant evening, Charles found it remarkably so, but I cannot tell why unless the absence of Miss Terry – towards whom his conscience reproaches him with now being perfectly indifferent – was a relief to him. . . . There were only twelve dances, of which I danced nine, and was merely prevented from dancing the rest by the want of a partner. . . . There were very few beauties and such as there were were not very handsome . . . The Miss Maitlands are both prettyish; very like Anne; with brown skins, large dark eyes, and a good deal of nose. The General has got the gout, and Mrs Maitland the jaundice. Miss Debary, Susan and Sally all in black . . . made their appearance; and I was as civil to them as their bad breath would allow me.

James Digweed left Hampshire today. I think he must be in love with you, from his anxiety to go to the Faversham Balls, and likewise from his supposing that the two elms fell from their grief at your absence. Was not it a gallant idea? It never occurred to me before, but I daresay it was so.

The sunny security of the Austens' existence at the close of the eighteenth century was broken by one jarring and surprising incident. One afternoon in August 1799, the rich and respectable Mrs Leigh Perrot was leaving a shop in Bath where she had purchased a packet of black lace: she was stopped by the shopman, who accused her of taking with it some white lace which she had not paid for. Opening the packet, she discovered the white lace was there and handed it back, explaining that there had been some mistake. Since she was very rich and the lace worth only a few shillings, it should have been clear that she was speaking the truth; but the shopman refused to believe her and laid an information against her with a magistrate. Some days later she was taken off to the local prison at Ilchester. A prison in those days was a place of Hogarthian horror of a kind that an elderly gentlewoman like Mrs Leigh Perrot had never been in sight of: brutal, filthy, sordid. Mr Leigh Perrot however persuaded the jailer to lodge her in his house till the time of her trial; this might mean a stay of several months. The jailer's lodgings, though better than the prison,

(above) James Leigh Perrot,
brother to Jane Austen's mother

(right) Jane, Mrs James Leigh Perrot

were poky and dirty enough to depress the Leigh Perrots; and their spirits were not lightened by the knowledge that in those days stealing anything over the value of five shillings was a capital offence for which, if convicted, Mrs Leigh Perrot could be at worst hanged and at best transported for fourteen years to Botany Bay. Why she was ever accused is a mystery: the most probable explanation is that the shopman, a known bad character and in financial difficulties, calculated that the rich Mr Leigh Perrot would be ready to pay him a large sum to withdraw his accusation. Mr Leigh Perrot however soon let it be understood that he would never submit to blackmail of this kind. He comes out of the story as likable and admirable as was his sister Mrs Austen. He had made up his mind that, if his wife was to be transported, he would sell all his property and go with her. Meanwhile he settled down to spend the next few months with her in the jailer's house, confined to a small dirty sitting room, often made noisy by the jailer's dirty children, and eating unappetizing meals cooked and served, as he saw with his own eyes, in disgusting conditions. At last on 29 March 1800, Mrs Leigh Perrot came up for trial. She was immediately and triumphantly acquitted. The story throws an unexpected light on the England of the period. On the one hand, it shows how a life as civilized as that of the Austens existed cheek by jowl with a legal system, cruel, inefficient and unjust; on the other, that this system was administered with a sort of ruthless fairness; so that all Mr Leigh Perrot's wealth and respectability could not save his wife from its severity, once its machinery had got into action.

Meanwhile the Austen family had rallied round their unfortunate relations with words of sympathy and offers of help. Mr and Mrs Austen suggested that Jane and Cassandra should go and stay with their aunt in prison to be companions to her; also that they should support her in court at her trial. Mrs Leigh Perrot firmly refused both offers: the jailer's house, she said, was no place for gently brought up young women and 'to have two young creatures gazed at in a public court would cut me to the very heart!' This refusal is to her credit; the Austens' offer is also much to theirs. It shows that they thought it wrong that their daughters should be spared the sight of life's harsher, uglier sides, if this meant failing to comfort and help their uncle and aunt, when they were in trouble.

(above) Duck shooting, by G. Morland, 1790
(below) Hare shooting, by G. Morland, 1790

(overleaf) The Bridges over the Canal in Sydney Gardens, Bath

4

Bath

Jane Austen was now twenty-five years old and hitherto her life had been a happy one. Not so happy as to make her unnaturally ignorant of the ills which mortal flesh is heir to: if she had not suffered from these herself, people close to her had. Her eldest brother's wife had died soon after marriage; her sister's fiancé had been struck down by a mortal illness; her aunt had nearly been transported to Botany Bay; her cousin's husband had been guillotined. Further, she had felt the anxiety that came from knowing that her two sailor brothers were often in danger fighting for their country. But these troubles had been more than outbalanced by the fact that, blessed by nature with a bright intelligence and cheerful disposition, she had passed her days in a countryside that delighted her and in the company of relations she loved and appreciated and who loved and appreciated her. Finally her circumstances, mental and physical, were such as to help and encourage the development of her genius: and, if her books had as yet failed to find a publisher, she had the satisfaction of knowing that her father and sister, the two people whose opinion she valued most, enjoyed them very much. Altogether, the music of time, which accompanied this first phase of Jane Austen's life, was pitched pretty consistently in the major key.

Now she was to enter into a second phase, lasting eight or nine years, which, though not catastrophic, was, by contrast with what had gone before, in a minor key; for it was marked by several events which cast a growing shadow over its otherwise equable course. The first of these events occurred late in November 1800, when the Austen sisters were away staying with the Lloyds at Ibthorpe. Suddenly for some unrecorded reason – it may have been Mrs Austen's increasing ill health – Mr Austen decided, without waiting to

Sydney Gardens, Bath

consult any other member of the family, to retire and leave Steventon, where he had lived for over thirty years. His daughters came home to be met by their mother. 'Well girls!' she said abruptly, 'it is all settled; we have decided to leave Steventon and go to Bath.' Overcome by shock, Jane fainted dead away. This reaction is unlike anything else related of her and, for that reason, very revealing. It shows how overwhelmingly strong was a love of home and countryside that could compel her to a display of emotion so contrary to the habits of a lifetime and that, beneath her apparent composure, she was no less hypersensitive and high-strung than are most creative artists. This is further to be inferred by the fact that, though Cassandra was on a visit to Godmersham during the next month and that it was Jane's unbroken habit regularly to correspond with her when she was away, no letters from this time survive. They must surely have been among those that Cassandra destroyed as disclosing painful and intimate emotions that she knew Jane would not have wanted other people to read about.

It was not long however before her natural good spirits and her rational belief in making the best of things reasserted themselves. Writing to Cassandra at the beginning of January 1801, Jane has dismissed her regrets and found reasons to look forward to life in Bath.

> I get more and more reconciled to the idea of our removal. We have lived long enough in this neighbourhood, the Basingstoke Balls are certainly on the decline, there is something interesting in the bustle of going away, and the prospect of spending future summers by the sea or in Wales is very delightful. For a time we shall now possess many of the advantages which I have often thought of with envy in the wives of sailors and soldiers. It must not be generally known however that I am not sacrificing a great deal in quitting the country – or I can expect to inspire no tenderness, no interest in those we leave behind.

The family were not ready to leave till May. During part of the intervening months, Cassandra was away staying with Edward in Kent and Henry in London. Jane's letters to her are mostly about practical matters: what part of Bath they should live in, which of the family possessions they should take with them, and which to leave behind to be sold. Now and again her pages are brightened by a bit of local gossip: 'Eliza has seen Lord Craven at Barton . . . she found his presence very pleasing indeed, the little flaw of having a mistress now living with him at Ashdown Park seems to be the only unpleasing circumstance about him'; and by accounts of farewell visits to and from persons in the neighbourhood: 'Hardly a day passes in which we do not have some visit or other; yesterday came Mrs Bramstone, who is very sorry she is to lose us and afterwards Mr Holder who was shut up for an hour with my father and James in a most awful manner.' These words are in her cheerful mischievous Elizabeth Bennet tone. But was she always feeling like this? I find myself recalling another of her heroines and fancying that, in her last walks round the Steventon lanes and hedgerows, heavy with memories for her, she was in the tender pensive mood that she was later to picture as experienced by Anne Elliot taking her last walks round Kellynch and Upper Cross.

The months passed: Jane went for a farewell stay with the Bigg-Withers at Manydown; the Austen brothers called to say goodbye to their old home; all except James, who was to succeed his father as rector of Steventon. The first week of May saw Jane and her mother – Cassandra and her father were to follow later – driving into Bath on a fine afternoon to stay with the Leigh-Perrots while they looked for a house. For once Jane Austen does not praise good weather.

The first view of Bath [she wrote] I find does not answer my expectations; I think I see more distinctly through rain. The sun was got behind everything, and the appearance of the place from the top of Kingsdown was all vapour, shadow, smoke and confusion.

Bath: 'the world of the country gentry'

She did not however allow this first unfavourable impression to put her off the place or weaken her determination to find life there as enjoyable as possible. This did not prove difficult; she found much to entertain her there. Bath had ceased to be as fashionable as it had been fifty years earlier: the smart set of London had begun to prefer Regency Brighton. But Jane Austen's own world, the world of the country gentry, remained loyal to Bath. It was to Bath they crowded for some urban relaxation and amusement; by night at the theatre or at balls and concerts at the Upper or Lower Assembly Rooms; by day, meeting their friends at the Pump Room, going on expeditions to neighbouring beauty spots, walking the streets to inspect the new fashions at the milliner's or new songs at the music shop or new novels at the bookseller's. Jane Austen was not so excited by these varied delights as ten years earlier and partook of them more sparingly. But she was still able to get a great deal of fun out of them. Her first letters to Cassandra from Bath are among the most amusing she ever wrote. Already she knew a number of people there; within a week, and in intervals of house-hunting, she found time to note the new fashions: 'Black gauze cloaks are worn as much as anything', to attend balls and card parties, to go on walks to Weston and Lycombe and to be taken driving in his phaeton by a new admirer called Evelyn, whom she speaks of with more kindness than enthusiasm. 'I really believe he is very harmless,' she says, 'People do not seem afraid of him here and he gets groundsel for his birds and all that.' These various activities gave her the opportunity to study her fellow men and women and to write about them to Cassandra.

> In the evening I hope you honoured my toilette and ball with a thought, I dressed myself as well as I could and had all my finery much admired at home. By nine o'clock my uncle, aunt and I entered the rooms and linked Miss Winstone on to us. Before tea, it was rather a dull affair; but then the before tea did not last long, for there was only one dance, danced by four couples. Think of four couples, surrounded by about one hundred people, dancing in the upper rooms at Bath! After tea we cheered up; the breaking up of private parties sent some scores more to the ball and tho' it was shockingly and inhumanly thin for this place, there were people enough I suppose to have made five or six very pretty Basingstoke Assemblies. I then got Mr Evelyn to talk to, and Miss Twistleton to look at; and I am proud to say that I have a very good eye at an Adulteress, for tho' repeatedly assured that another in the party was SHE, I fixed upon the right one from the first. A resemblance to Mrs Leigh was my guide. She is not so pretty as I expected; her face has the same defect of baldness as her sister's, and her features not so handsome; she was highly rouged, and looked rather quietly and contentedly silly than anything else. Mrs Badcock and two

(*above and overleaf*) *The Pump Room, Bath*

young women were of the same party, except when Mrs Badcock thought herself obliged to leave them to run round the room after her drunken husband. His avoidance, and her pursuit with the probable intoxication of both, was an amusing scene.

Jane's news was not always cheerful. A daughter of some friends of the family called Mapleton died; Jane wrote to tell Cassandra about it.

You will be sorry to hear that Marianne Mapleton's disorder has ended fatally; she was believed out of danger on Sunday, but a sudden relapse carried her off the next day. So affectionate a family must suffer severely; and many a girl on early death has been praised into an angel, I believe, on slighter pretensions to beauty, sense and merit than Marianne.

These sentences add a little more to our knowledge of Jane Austen. Since it is to Cassandra that she is speaking about death, she is not constrained into any sort of formality, as she was when condoling with Philadelphia Walter. But so emotionally charged a subject still makes her a little shy and she hides this by expressing her admiration for the dead girl in a tone of graceful, ironic understatement.

Meanwhile – delightful excitement – a letter has come from Charles, saying that his ship has taken part in a successful engagement with a privateer for which he himself has been rewarded with £40 of prize money: he adds that he has spent some of this on topaz crosses with gold chains as presents for his sisters. That their 'particular little brother' should have remembered them and in this generous fashion touched Jane deeply. 'What avail is it to take prizes if he lays out the produce in presents to his sisters!' she exclaims to Cassandra, 'I shall write again to thank and reproach him – we shall be unbearably fine.' So Fanny Price, yet another heroine of hers, was to feel when her sailor brother William presented her with a similar cross.

II

June saw parents and daughters reunited and settled at No. 4 Sydney Place; they were to move later to Green Park Buildings. In the summer of 1801 they went for a seaside holiday to Sidmouth. Their stay there was marked by an event of extreme, perhaps of crucial, importance in Jane Austen's history. Largely for this reason, it is one of which we know almost nothing, only what can be gathered from a few brief remarks made, at various times towards the end of her life, by Cassandra to her nephews and nieces. Even these remarks, as

Sidmouth, Devon

reported to posterity, do not completely agree with one another. All we can be reasonably sure of is that at Sidmouth Jane met a young gentleman who showed signs of being extremely attracted by her. We do not know his name nor his profession, though there is a suggestion that he was a clergyman. We do know that he was handsome, intelligent and possessed of unusual charm; so much so that Cassandra, who hardly ever praised anybody, praised him warmly and even thought him good enough for her sister Jane. Jane thought so too. Cassandra judged them both to be seriously in love. But, before this love had openly declared itself and after they had only known each other for two or three weeks, the nameless gentleman was forced by some unbreakable engagement to leave Sidmouth. It was understood that he would soon come back and join the family again. Cassandra had no doubt that he would then state his intentions and that Jane would receive them favourably. He said goodbye. The next thing they heard of him was a letter from his brother saying that he had suddenly died. That is all. There are no letters from Jane for many months; no doubt, if there were, Cassandra had again destroyed them.

Jane's unhappiness, however, may account for another episode that took place more than a year later. In November 1802 the sisters were back at Steventon Rectory staying with their brother James; from there they left for a visit to their old friends the Bigg-Withers at Manydown. What was the surprise of Mr and Mrs James Austen on a Friday morning a day or two later to see the Bigg-Withers' carriage drive up to their front door. Out of it and into their hall came the Miss Austens and the Miss Bigg-Withers, all of them agitated and in tears. Still agitated and tearful, the Miss Bigg-Withers em-braced the Miss Austens, climbed back into their carriage and drove off. Immediately Jane and Cassandra turned to James Austen and, without any explanation, said that they must go back to Bath at once and – since in those days it was not considered possible for young ladies to travel alone in a public conveyance – they must ask James to come with them. This meant that he would not be able to get back home in time to take the Sunday services: he therefore suggested that they should wait till Monday. Ordinarily, they would certainly have agreed. To stop a clergyman, and him their own brother, from performing his Sunday duties was the kind of act they most disapproved of. But this time they brushed his words aside and insisted. During the journey, James learned their reason. It seemed that the night before Mr Bigg-Wither's son and heir, the twenty-one-year-old Harris Bigg-Wither, had proposed to Jane and been accepted. Next morning she had come down and broken the engagement off. The incident had left her so upset as to feel that she could not bear to stay in the neighbourhood even for a night.

After this, the impenetrable curtain of Cassandra's discretion descends: we have no letters from Jane for over a year. However, taking the two episodes together and considering what we know of her later feelings and opinions, we can allow ourselves to have a guess at the course of her emotional life during these two years. It looks as if she had been thoroughly in love at Sidmouth, more, so far as we know, than at any other time in her life. But the romance had been so short and so frustrated that, by the end of the following year, she had judged herself enough recovered to contemplate marrying someone else. There were good reasons for her doing so. She was now twenty-seven years old, a late age to be married in those days: and marriage then was the only career open to women in her walk of life, the only one that appeared to offer an opportunity for an active and satisfying existence. It was especially desirable for the Miss Austens, since their father had little money to leave them; so that there was a serious possibility of their being destined for a narrow empty future as penurious spinsters. 'Single women have a dreadful propensity to be poor,' Jane with a rueful smile was to say later. No doubt she would not be marrying Harris Bigg-Wither for love in the romantic sense of the word; but marriage then was not regarded as a culmination of a romance but as a social arrangement for the promotion and maintenance of the family. As such, however, it did involve solemn obligations and a woman should not enter into it for selfish or worldly reasons: she should be sure that she is marrying a man for whom she could feel respect and affection. Jane Austen might have felt them for Harris Bigg-Wither, who had the reputation of an excellent character, and whose sisters were among her dearest friends. Added to this, he was a man of fortune and position which would enable him to help her parents in their old age; Cassandra too, should she remain unmarried. Finally he lived in a countryside for which Jane felt a lifelong and peculiar affection. It is true he was six or seven years younger than her: but if he did not mind this, there is no reason why she should.

Yet when it came to the point, Jane found that she could not go through with the engagement. This surely must mean that, though she had not realized it, the flame of her love for the Sidmouth gentleman was still so much alight that she could not help comparing her two suitors. This comparison made it impossible for her to marry Harris Bigg-Wither. Years later, writing to her niece Fanny, she was to say that nothing could exceed the misery of being bound to one while preferring another. At Manydown meanwhile, she was discovering already the truth she was to state so poignantly in her last novel *Persuasion*: namely that women have a sad ability to go on loving when hope is gone. Jane Austen's nature, though not passionate, was the opposite of shallow. The impact of her brief romance at Sidmouth had proved a great deal deeper than she had foreseen.

Was it a lasting impact? In some ways it seems to have been. The tone in which she speaks of true love in her later books and letters – though never so solemn as to exclude an occasional smile – is more tender and thoughtful than it is in her earlier. Moreover she never married and this may have been because she never got the chance of marrying anyone who attracted her as the Sidmouth gentleman had done. All the same, his effect on her should not be exaggerated. A three weeks' acquaintance which had not had time to lead to an engagement is hardly enough to have broken her heart irremediably or revolutionized her attitude to love and marriage. Nor did it: the tone in which she speaks of these subjects may alter a little with the years, but her opinion on them did not. They remain those of the realistic pre-romantic eighteenth century and of her own realistic pre-romantic point of view. Many years later in *Persuasion* she describes Anne Elliot continuing to love a man when hope is apparently gone; but she says that she could have loved again, if she had had the opportunity of meeting a man able to inspire her to do so. 'No second attachment,' she comments, 'the only thoroughly natural, happy and sufficient cure, at her time of life, had been possible to the nice tone of her mind, the fastidiousness of her taste, in the small limits of the society around them.' The phrase 'at her time of life' makes one pause: at the time of her disappointment in love Anne Elliot was ten years younger than Jane Austen. This may suggest that Jane felt at thirty she was too old to fall in love again. But, since according to the ideas of the time, love in this sense was not essential to marriage and esteem was enough to take its place, it looks as if poor Harris Bigg-Wither could not even inspire enough esteem to drive the memory of Jane's Sidmouth suitor from her heart. Still she must have fancied he might be able to or she would not have accepted him. The death of the Sidmouth suitor had not proved an undying grief.

III

This was partly the combined effect of time and good sense. But there was a stronger and more significant reason for it. Once again we must remember her twofold nature, the fact that she was an artist as well as a woman. Man feels satisfied in so far as he is fulfilling his creative instinct: a great artist like Jane Austen finds this fulfilment primarily in her art. In fact, soon after the Manydown episode Jane Austen was once more occupied in literary activities. First of all, presumably encouraged by her father, she sent off *Northanger Abbey*, under its first title of *Susan*, to another publisher called Crosby. Unlike Cadell, he did not refuse to read it: instead he wrote promising to publish it fairly soon and offering to pay £10 on account in the meantime. Having done this much, he put the manuscript in a drawer and left it there for several years. This second failure to get her books published cannot but have increased Jane Austen's sense of frustration and consequent depression. Meanwhile she had also started a new novel, that, which in its unfinished form, was to make its appearance long after her death under the title of *The Watsons*. There is not much of it and, though it contains scenes that show Jane Austen at her best, the general effect, judged by the standard set by her finished works, is unequal. This inequality throws a light on her methods. The texture of the writing is not so continuously lively as in the finished works and the beginning, in particular, is all too obviously a piece of exposition. We conclude from these facts that she started with drawing a skeleton outline and then went on to give it life and character by a careful process of enriching and refining. *The Watsons* also suggests – and this was to be expected – that its author was graver than when she wrote her earlier novels. The comedy is less high-spirited, the satire directed less against silliness and affectation and more against serious moral defects: Tom Musgrave's snobbish selfishness, the squabbling ill-nature of Margaret and Penelope Watson, competing with each other to capture a husband. This graver tone is emphasized by the fact that not only is the hero a clergyman – so also was the hero of *Northanger Abbey* – but he is praised for specifically clerical virtues and because he preached sermons which were genuine aids to devotion. Thus, casually and as it were unintentionally, Jane Austen makes the reader aware of those religious convictions in which her moral preferences were rooted. The events of her life had led her to think more about them so that they showed themselves more in her works.

Fate and Cassandra have preserved no letters from 1802 to 1803; but we do know that in 1803 and before her disastrous stay at Manydown Jane was away from Bath on visits to Dawlish and Teignmouth and Ramsgate. She went to Ramsgate to meet a proposed new addition to her family. Frank Austen was back in England for a period on half-pay to help organize the sea-fencibles, a body of men recruited to keep a look-out on the coast and to give the alarm, should Napoleon try to land an army in England. While there, he became engaged to a Miss Mary Gibson. Jane and Cassandra were disappointed; they had hoped he might marry Martha Lloyd and this in spite of the fact that her sister Mary had proved a disappointment as a sister-in-law. This did not stop them taking very much to Mary Gibson when they had met her. Indeed the marriage was to prove very happy. It did not take place till 1806, partly because Frank could not afford it and partly because he was soon ordered back to sea again, to remain there for much of the next two years. He wrote his fiancée regular and lengthy letters, characteristically full of precise facts and with an occasional touch of sardonic humour. As was to be expected from an

Austen, his expressions of affection are rare and restrained; but he shows his feelings by treating Mary Gibson as an intellectual equal to whom it is right and natural he should confide his views on the conduct of the naval campaign and all his personal hopes and disappointments. These included one big disappointment. His squadron had been hanging about the Mediterranean many months hoping to get a chance of taking part in an important naval engagement. In 1805 it looked as if one would take place, but alas without their help. He wrote to Mary:

> As I have no doubt but the event would be highly honourable to our arms, and be at the same time productive of some good prizes, I shall have to lament our absence on such an occasion on a double account, the loss of pecuniary advantage as well as of professional credit. . . . You, perhaps, may not feel this so forcibly as I do, and in your satisfaction at my having avoided the danger of battle may not much regret my losing the credit of having contributed to gain a victory; not so myself!
>
> I do not profess to like fighting for its own sake, but if there have been an action with the combined fleets I shall ever consider the day on which I sailed from the squadron as the most inauspicious one of my life.

His fears were justified. Frank Austen had the bad luck to miss no less an action than the Battle of Trafalgar. He was acutely disappointed and told Mary so. But his Austen self-control soon reasserted itself. He ended his letter to her:

> To lose all share in the glory of a day which surpasses all which ever went before, is what I cannot think of with any degree of patience, but, as I cannot write upon that subject without complaining, I will drop it for the present, till time and reflection reconcile me a little more to what I know is now inevitable.

Some days later he had got over his disappointment enough to be much interested in meeting Villeneuve, Admiral of the defeated French Fleet and now a prisoner on the British flagship, *Euryalus*. Frank observed him with something of his sister Jane's amused curiosity.

> I was on board the *Euryalus* yesterday [he wrote to Mary Gibson] and was introduced to the French Admiral Villeneuve, who is a prisoner there. He appears to be about forty-five years of age, of dark complexion, with rather an unmeaning countenance, and has not much the appearance of a gentleman. He is, however, so much of a Frenchman as to bear his misfortunes with cheerfulness.

English Men of War, of the period

Frank Austen was mistaken in his last judgment: six months later, overcome with shame at his defeat, Villeneuve killed himself. Perhaps the Austens were too English to understand foreigners.

IV

The Battle of Trafalgar happened in 1805, two years later than our last sight of Jane Austen. Little seems to have happened to her in 1804; possibly in this year Mrs Austen fell seriously ill. She was restored to health by the skill of Mr Bowen and by the devoted nursing of her two daughters. Her cure left her in a state of mingled gratitude and high spirits which required verse for its expression:

> Says Death, 'I've been trying these three weeks and more
> To seize an old Madam here at Number Four,
> Yet I still try in vain, tho' she's turned of three score;
> To what is my ill success owing?

I'll tell you, old Fellow, if you cannot guess
To what you're indebted for your ill success –
To the prayers of my husband, whose love I possess,
To the care of my daughters, whom Heaven will bless,
To the skill and attention of Bowen.

These lines help to bring Mrs Austen to life to us; they illustrate a gaiety of spirit which at sixty years old – sixty meant old age in those days – led her to celebrate her recovery from what might have been a mortal illness by writing comic verses about it. It also shows how fond she was of her daughters and they of her.

If 1804 was the year of her illness, she was well enough in September to go with her husband and Jane – Cassandra was on a visit to Weymouth – for a holiday to Lyme Regis. Here, for the first time for two years, we hear Jane's voice in a letter to Cassandra and speaking once again in cheerful tones. She gives the news about lodgings and servants – they had an excellent manservant with them called James, to whom she had lent *Robinson Crusoe* – about a letter from Charles away at sea, about new acquaintances and walks on the Cobb, where she was later to imagine Louisa Musgrove's dramatic accident, about some enjoyable sea bathing, about a ball at the local Assembly Rooms.

The Ball last night was pleasant, but not full for Thursday. My father staid very contentedly till half past nine (we went a little after eight) and then walked home with James and a lanthorn, though I believe the lanthorn may sometimes be a great inconvenience to him. My mother and I staid about an hour later. Nobody asked me the two first dances; the two next I danced with Mr Cranford, and had I chosen to stay longer might have danced with Mr Granville, Mrs Granville's son whom my dear friend Miss Armstrong offered to introduce to me, or with a new odd-looking man who had been eyeing me for some time, and at last without any introduction, asked me if I meant to dance again. I think he must be Irish by his ease, and because I imagine him to belong to the hon[bl] Barnwalls, who are the son, and son's wife of an Irish viscount, bold queer-looking people, just fit to be quality at Lyme. I called yesterday morning (ought it not in strict propriety to be termed yester morning?) on Miss Armstrong and was introduced to her father and mother. Like other young ladies, she is considerably genteeler than her parents. . . . We afterwards walked for an hour on the Cobb; she is very conversable in a common way; I do not perceive wit or genius, but she has sense and some degree of taste, and her manners are very engaging. She seems to like people rather too easily: she thought the Downes pleasant . . .

Lyme Regis

The scenery of Lyme and its surroundings is at its best in a fine autumn and Jane Austen responded to it. Tranquillizing and refreshing, its beauty lingered on in memory to be recalled in *Persuasion* twelve years later in enthusiastic words which well convey the quality and strength of her feeling for nature. Particularly she delighted in the scenery around Charmouth with 'its sweet retired bay backed by dark cliffs, where fragments of low rock among the sands make it the happiest spot for watching the flow of the tide, for sitting in unwearied contemplation'.

V

Back at Bath the clouds began to gather again and darker than before. Indeed the next twelve months must have been some of the saddest of Jane Austen's not very sad life. The sadness was occasioned by two deaths. First on 18 December 1804 came news that on the 16th, Jane's own birthday, Mrs Lefroy, out riding, had fallen off her horse and been killed. Since Jane had been living

in Bath, the two friends cannot have seen each other often. But Mrs Lefroy had kept a special place in Jane's heart. She had made an impression on it at an age when it was most impressionable; she had encouraged her, when it was most important she should be encouraged. Because of this, her death came as a special shock. How much Jane Austen felt it is shown by the fact that four years later, on her thirty-third birthday and the anniversary of Mrs Lefroy's accident, she was moved to write a poem. Here are some lines from it:

> The day returns again, my natal day;
> What mixed emotions in my mind arise!
> Beloved Friend; four years have passed away
> Since thou wert snatched for ever from our eyes.
>
> The day commemorative of my birth,
> Bestowing life, and light, and hope to me
> Brings back the hour which was thy last on earth.
> O! bitter pang of torturing memory!

> Angelic woman! past my power to praise
>   In language meet thy talents, temper, mind,
> Thy solid worth, thy captivating grace,
>   Thou friend and ornament of human kind.
>
> But come, fond Fancy, thou indulgent power;
>   Hope is desponding, chill, severe, to thee:
> Bless thou this little portion of an hour
>   Let me behold her as she used to be.
>
> I see her here with all her smiles benign,
>   Her looks of eager love, her accents sweet,
> That voice and countenance almost divine,
>   Expression, harmony, alike complete. . .
>
> Hers is the energy of soul sincere;
>   Her Christian spirit, ignorant to feign,
> Seek but to comfort, heal, enlighten, cheer,
>   Confer a pleasure or prevent a pain.
>
> Can aught enhance such goodness? yes to me
>   Her partial favour from my earliest years
> Consummates all: ah! give me but to see
>   Her smile of love! The vision disappears. . .

These lines are Jane Austen's only attempt at a serious poem. It cannot be said that it is a success judged as poetry. Hers was a prose genius: her sense of words and rhythm deserted her when she attempted the heightened mode of verse. But a heightened mode is a natural way of expressing heightened feelings; and the fact that she chose to write in verse is evidence of how strong Jane's affection for Mrs Lefroy had been. She felt that, if she were to express it adequately, she must write in verse.

Next month brought a worse blow. On 2 January 1805 Jane Austen wrote to her brother Captain Francis Austen on board HMS *Leopard* in harbour at Portsmouth:

My Dearest Frank,

   I wrote to you yesterday; but your letter to Cassandra this morning, by which we learn the probability of your being by this time at Portsmouth,

Laura Place, Bath

obliges me to write to you again, having unfortunately a communication as necessary as painful to make to you. Your affectionate heart will be greatly wounded, and I wish the shock could have been lessened by a better preparation; but the event has been sudden, and so must be the information of it. We have lost an excellent Father. An illness of only eight and forty hours carried him off yesterday morning between ten and eleven. He was seized on Saturday with a return of the feverish complaint, which he had been subject to for the three last years; evidently a more violent attack from the first, as the application which had before produced almost immediate relief, seemed for some time to afford him scarcely any. On Sunday however he was much better, so much so as to make Bowen quite easy, and give us every hope of his being well again in a few days. But these hopes gradually gave way as the day advanced, and when Bowen saw him at ten that night he was greatly alarmed. A Physician was called in yesterday morning, but he was at that time past all possibility of cure and Doctor Gibbs and Mr Bowen had scarcely left the room before he sunk into a sleep from which he never woke. Everything I trust and believe was done for him that was possible! It has been very sudden! Within twenty four hours of his death he was walking with only the help of a stick, was even reading! We had however some hours of preparation, and when we understood his recovery to be hopeless, most fervently did we pray for the speedy release which ensued. To have seen him languishing long, struggling for hours, would have been dreadful! and thank God! we were spared from it. Except the restlessness and confusion of high fever, he did not suffer – and he was mercifully spared from knowing that he was about to quit the Objects so beloved, so fondly cherished as his wife and children ever were. His tenderness as a father, who can do justice to? My mother is tolerably well, she bears up with great fortitude, but I fear her health must suffer under such a shock. An express was sent for James, and he arrived here this morning before eight o'clock. The funeral is to be on Saturday, at Walcot Church. The serenity of the Corpse is most delightful! It preserves the sweet, benevolent smile which always distinguished him. . . .

> We all unite in Love, and I am affectionately
> Yours
> Jane Austen.

This letter retains the eighteenth-century manner. But this time Jane Austen feels so strongly as to forget her shyness about expressing emotion: her tender love for her father, her affectionate anxiety to save Frank from the shock of sudden bad news, make themselves felt poignantly and unselfconsciously, for all that they are expressed in formal phrasing and measured sentences. Indeed, though she dwells characteristically on anything that may soften the harshness of the family's grief – relief that Mr Austen did not know that he was dying and that his end came peacefully – his death was inevitably a great sorrow to her. She had lost not only a loving and lovable parent – 'the loss of such a parent must be felt or we should be brutes,' she exclaimed in another letter to Frank – but also the person who had done most to foster her literary sense and encourage her writing.

At first, too, it looked as if his death would be a considerable misfortune in a material sense. The greater part of George Austen's income had died with him: poor Mrs Austen, from being the wife of the head of a relatively prosperous family, was suddenly reduced to the status of a widow, faced with the dreary prospect of having to support herself and two grown-up daughters on an income of £210 per year. However her sons were affectionate, dutiful and active; they rallied round. James consulted with Henry and Henry wrote to Edward as to what could be done for their mother and sisters. James and Henry each volunteered to give her £50 per year to which the richer Edward added £100. Finally, Frank, in spite of the fact that his income tended to vary much more than did those of his brothers, wrote offering his mother another £100 a year: he asked that Mrs Austen should not be told of his contribution presumably because she might then hesitate to accept it. However Henry, who was noted in the family for his indiscretion, did tell her and she did refuse to take more than £50. Even so, owing to her sons' generosity, her annual income now amounted to something like £460 per year. In 1805 this meant she was, if not rich, relatively comfortable, able to keep at least one living-in servant, with enough free money for her and each of her daughters to afford an occasional visit to their friends and relations. 'Never were children so good as mine!' cried Mrs Austen.

The Reverend George Austen (1731–1805)

5

Southampton

Nevertheless her way of life was narrower and less agreeable than it had been. It was also unsettled and was to remain so for some years. To begin with she stayed on in Bath: Mrs Austen liked the idea of living in the same town as her affectionate brother, Mr Leigh Perrot. The better to suit their reduced circumstances, she and her daughters moved to cheaper lodgings first in Gay Street and later in Trim Street. In April 1805 they were joined by Martha Lloyd. Her mother had died leaving her homeless; and the Austens had asked her to make her home with them. This act of friendship on their part turned out later in the year to be of practical advantage to them. In the autumn, Cassandra and Jane were invited to stay in Kent with their brother Edward. In the ordinary way one of them would have had to refuse in order that Mrs Austen should not be left alone. Now Martha Lloyd was there to keep her company instead.

Earlier in the year and before Mrs Lloyd had died, Cassandra had visited the Lloyds in Hampshire. Jane's letters to her help us to guess something of her state of mind and spirits at this stage in her life. I have to say guess; for she talks about herself as little as ever. Like those of the past, these letters are made up of news and gossip, livened with an occasional entertaining turn of phrase; as when she speaks of Mr Bendish 'who seems nothing but a tall young man' or reports that the youngest Miss Whiteley 'has come to be grown-up and have a fine complexion and wear a great square muslin shawl'. The general impression made by these letters however is more dispirited than that of her earlier correspondence. Humorous comments are rare and there are none of her old outbursts of impish mischief, nothing to shock the most sensitive of later critics. At times it even seems as if she is feeling depressed but shrinks from owning up to it, because she thinks no good will come of doing so. Thus in the midst of telling Cassandra the Bath news, she will break off to exclaim about old Mrs Lloyd's illness: 'Poor woman! may her end be peaceful and easy as the exit we have witnessed! and I dare say it will'; she then goes on to resume her Bath chronicle with a sentence of apology. 'The nonsense I have written in this and in my last letter seems out of place at such a time; but I will not mind it, it will do you no harm.' This is said with a smile; but it is a rueful smile, as of one who faces life without the glad hopefulness of the past. Indeed Jane Austen had less to be hopeful about. The sadness induced by bereavement and disappointment in love was increased by the prospect of having little to look forward to, at least for the time being. One effect of this was slightly to soften the tone in which she spoke of people she found tiresome or ridiculous. 'Poor Mrs Stent! it has been her lot to be always in the way; but we must be merciful, perhaps in time we may come to be Mrs Stents ourselves, unequal to anything and unwelcome to everybody.' This thought would not have occurred to her ten years earlier. It suggests that she had grown less confident and more despondent.

Despondency may account for the significant fact that for the first time for years she appears to have stopped writing. She did not go on with *The Watsons*; indeed she dropped it for ever. She never said why, but one of her nephews, writing after her death, suggests that it was because Emma Watson, the heroine, was, as he oddly puts it, 'in a position of poverty and obscurity which, though not necessarily connected with vulgarity, had a sad tendency to degenerate into it'. I cannot believe that this was the true reason: Emma Watson's family was no poorer than that of Fanny Price and socially at least as high. Moreover she herself was later in the story to be courted by the heir to a peerage, a more exalted prospect than was offered to any of Jane Austen's other heroines. Mr Darcy may, in the triumphant words of Mrs Bennet, have been 'as good as a lord', but Emma Watson's suitor actually was a lord. The reason why in later years Jane Austen never went on with *The Watsons* remains unknown; but it looks as if at first she put it aside because worry and anxiety about the future had for the time being disturbed the tranquillity of mind she needed to concentrate on composition; and that successive moves involved her in so many distracting practical activities as to leave her little time for anything else.

II

For she was not to stay in Bath. She did not want to; she had grown actively to dislike both the place and the life there. This is not surprising; they had appealed to Jane Austen when a girl curious to know the world and out to enjoy herself socially but not to Jane Austen, a woman of thirty, concerned to adjust herself to approaching middle age. Cassandra and Mrs Austen also wanted to leave Bath. Early in 1806, with a happy feeling of escape, they left; and, after a short stay at Clifton, moved to Southampton. Francis Austen and his newly married wife Mary were living there awaiting a new appointment at sea and suggested that his mother and sisters should come and share his home. Before joining them, they took the chance to pay a visit to a cousin of Mrs Austen's, the Reverend Thomas Leigh, a rector of Adlestrop in Gloucestershire. They had hardly arrived there before Mr Leigh got news that a remote cousin had died leaving him, it was thought, heir to the ancestral home of Stoneleigh Abbey in neighbouring Warwickshire, together with the large Stoneleigh estates. The wording of the will was ambiguous and Mr Leigh's lawyer thought it would be wise for him to take possession of Stoneleigh Abbey before other possible claimants had time to start disputing his right to it. Thither therefore, Mr Leigh and his guests immediately transferred themselves. This was the only occasion, so far as we know, that Jane Austen stayed at a great aristocratic country mansion and could observe the way of life there at first hand. She did not indeed see this way of life at its most magnificent: it was not as if she were staying with the Duke of Devonshire at Chatsworth or with Lord Lansdowne at Bowood. These belonged to the grand exclusive Whig aristocracy, the Leighs to the more countrified sections of the Tory aristocracy. Moreover, though Mr and Mrs Leigh were gentlemanly and ladylike, they had not themselves been brought up to the full aristocratic mode of living. All the same, staying with them at Stoneleigh Abbey was very different from staying with the Bigg-Withers at Manydown or the Lefroys at Ashe. For one thing the house was on the great scale, a vast spreading pile, the work of generations of Leighs and incorporating some remains of a medieval abbey, a large Elizabethan wing and a still larger one in majestic Palladian style, built in the middle of the eighteenth century. The whole was the setting for a stately traditional pattern of living. Let Mrs Austen describe her impression of the visit; she does it vividly in a letter to Steventon Rectory.

Here we found ourselves on Tuesday eating fish, venison, and all manner of good things, in a large and noble parlour, hung round with family portraits. The house is larger than I could have supposed. We cannot find our way about it – I mean the best part; as to the offices, which were the Abbey, Mr Leigh almost despairs of ever finding his way about them. I have proposed him setting up direction posts at the angles. I had expected to find everything about the place

Jane Austen. Watercolour by
Cassandra Austen, 1804

very fine and all that, but I had no idea of its being so beautiful. I had pictured to myself long avenues, dark rookeries, and dismal yew trees but here are no such dismal things. The Avon runs near the house, amidst green meadows, bounded by large and beautiful woods, full of delightful walks.

At nine in the morning we say our prayers in a handsome chapel, of which the pulpit, &c. &c. is now hung with black. Then follows breakfast, consisting of chocolate, coffee, and tea, plum cake, pound cake, hot rolls, cold rolls, bread and butter, and dry toast for me. The house steward, a fine large respectable-looking man, orders all these matters. The gardens contain four acres and a half. The ponds supply excellent fish, the park excellent venison; there is a great quantity of rabbits, pigeons, and all sorts of poultry. There is a delightful dairy, where is made butter, good Warwickshire cheese and cream ditto. One manser-vant is called the baker, and does nothing but brew and bake. The number of casks in the strong-beer cellar is beyond imagination. This is an odd sort of letter. I write just as things come into my head a bit now and a bit then . . .

She goes on to describe the house party which included some more Leigh relations, one of them a garrulous peeress called Lady Saye and Sele. 'We all seem to be in a good humour, disposed to be pleased and endeavouring to be agreeable, and I hope we succeed. Poor Lady Saye and Sele to be sure is rather tormenting, though sometimes amusing and affords Jane many a good laugh: but she fatigues me sadly.'

Jane Austen was not the first author to be amused at Lady Saye and Sele. Fanny Burney describes meeting her attired in a dress 'full of fine fancies and her head full of feathers and flowers and jewels and jee-gaws.'

I am very happy to see you [said Lady Saye and Sele to her]. I have longed to see you a great while: I have read your performance and am quite delighted with it! I think it is the most elegant novel I have ever read in my life. Such a style! – I'm sure I could never write a novel – I could not get a style – that's the thing – I could not tell how to get a style! and a novel's nothing without the style, you know!

If this was typical of Lady Saye and Sele's conversation, it is no wonder that she afforded Jane a good laugh. Mrs Austen's words also indicate that Jane was recovering from any loss of spirits she had suffered from in the last year.

A Post Captain at the time Jane Austen's
brothers were in the Royal Navy

The letter is illuminating as helping to make clear the place of the Austens in the hierarchy of English society. Unused though they were to the Stoneleigh scale of living, it did not induce in them any awkward sense of social inferiority. They felt at ease with the company they met there because, though poorer, they were broadly speaking their social equals, members of the upper as distinguished from the middle and lower ranks of society. Because Lady Saye and Sele was a relation, though a distant one, Mrs Austen speaks of her as she would have spoken of a county neighbour at Steventon, not as if a peeress was a being of a different species to herself.

Southampton

Her daughters would have spoken and felt the same. This is apparent in Jane's novels. She talks of class distinctions blithely and frankly and without any of the uneasy embarrassment that afflicts most subsequent English novelists when they tackle this distressing subject. This came from the unconscious confidence engendered in her by her own secure social position. It was also due to the fact that she lived in an age when class was taken for granted by herself and everyone she knew as a right and natural feature of any human society. But she was not a snob. She thought Darcy mistaken in hesitating to marry delightful Elizabeth Bennet because she had a vulgar mother and an uncle in trade and she laughed mercilessly at Sir Walter Elliot for thinking well of himself simply because he happened to be born with a title.

Autumn saw the Austens arrive at Southampton to be rejoined there by Martha Lloyd. The house they had rented sounds pleasant enough: roomy and old-fashioned with a big garden and situated in a corner of Castle Square under the shadow of the picturesque old city wall. It overlooked a miniature mock-gothic castle built by the Lord Lansdowne of the day for his wife, whom the Austens used to watch from their windows driving out in a pretty little equipage drawn by eight long-tailed ponies whose colour graduated from dark to pale brown, with the two leaders controlled by boy postillions in livery sitting astride them. For their first few months in Southampton, Jane Austen was to enjoy the company of Frank and his family. Frank was a very agreeable addition to domestic life, not only as a companion, but also for practical reasons. He was a keen and skilled handyman – this aspect of him, she said, suggested features in her portrait of Captain Harville in *Persuasion* – for ever at work putting up book-shelves or making fringes for the drawing room curtains. Alas, in the spring he was ordered to go to sea again; and his family left Southampton with him. This meant that his mother and sisters no longer had any close relation living near them. The result was that, though they stayed on at Southampton for three more years, they never struck root there and were always looking elsewhere for a permanent home.

III

For the time being they settled temporarily into a pattern of living. It was not all that different from their old pattern but quieter, in conformity with their greater age and changed circumstances. They still went in for some mild social life: paid calls, accepted invitations to dine and play cards, even attended an occasional ball at the local Assembly Rooms. But their engagements were fewer and, though they made one or two new friends, they avoided cultivating acquaintances who lived more expensively than they could afford to do.

One day Jane and Frank called on a Mrs Lance, to whom they had been given an introduction. Jane commented on the visit with amusement:

> We found only Mrs Lance at home, and whether she boasts any offspring besides a grand pianoforte did not appear. She was civil and chatty enough, and offered to introduce us to some acquaintances in Southampton, which was gratefully declined. I suppose they must be acting by the orders of Mr Lance of Netherton in this civility, as there seems no other reason for their coming near us. They will not come often, I dare say. They live in a handsome style and are rich, and she seemed to like to be rich, and we gave her to understand that we were far from being so; she will soon feel therefore that we are not worth her acquaintance.

More and more Jane's chief activities and favourite pleasures were to be found at home. For the first time in her correspondence she mentions the pleasures of solitude. In October 1808 she writes to tell Cassandra, who was away staying at Godmersham, that for some reason Martha Lloyd's return to Southampton may be delayed. 'If it does,' Jane adds, 'I shall not much regard it on my own account; for I am now got into a way of being alone that I shall not wish even for her.' For the rest she found enough to do helping to supervise the catering – 'You know how interesting the purchase of a sponge cake is to me,' she remarks to Cassandra – and concerning herself with the garden. Here her taste was shaped and coloured by her reading. She said she wanted a laburnum planted there and more especially a syringa because they recalled a favourite quotation from Cowper:

> Laburnum rich
> In streaming gold; syringa Iv'ry pure.

In the evening the ladies occupied themselves embroidering, playing card games – Brag and Speculation – and, following the tradition established by Mr Austen, reading aloud. Among the books Jane mentions as read during these years are *The Female Quixote*, a skit on Cervantes which she enjoyed, *Espriella* by Southey, a book purporting to describe England as seen through critical and foreign eyes. Jane's robust patriotism led her to dislike this: 'The man describes well,' she exclaims, 'but is horribly anti-English. He deserves to be the foreigner he assumes!' Even more did she dislike *Alphosine*, a novel by Madame de Genlis. Her disapproval was on moral grounds. *Alphosine* dealt sympathetically and sentimentally with the unpleasing subject of a woman who left her husband because her marriage had not been consummated and was later discovered asleep in the embraces of a page. 'Alphosine did not do,'

Jane said severely, 'we were disgusted in twenty pages, as, independent of a bad translation, it has indelicacies which disgrace a pen hitherto so pure.' Jane's severity may seem surprising considering that she was not prudish, at least if judged by Victorian standards. In her letters to Cassandra, she will allude to a gentleman keeping a mistress in a frank and even flippant tone, unthinkable, say, from Charlotte Brontë. This however was because she lived in a more outspoken age. It was all right, according to the conventions in which Jane Austen had been brought up, for a young lady to refer openly to kept mistresses, just as it was all right for her to refer openly to the fact that an acquaintance suffered from bad breath. But this did not mean that she approved of keeping a mistress any more than it meant that she did not dislike bad breath. In many ways indeed the eighteenth century was even more moralistic than the Victorian age. No Victorian novel moralizes so insistently as does *Clarissa Harlowe*, no Victorian sage is so dogmatically didactic as Jane Austen's 'dear Dr Johnson'.

Like his, her moral views were rooted in her religious convictions. She disapproved of adultery not merely for social reasons but because it was contrary to Christian morality. How significant is her reaction to the news that Mrs Powlett, a former Steventon neighbour, has eloped from her husband! 'This is a sad story about Mrs Powlett. I should not have suspected her of such a thing: she stayed for the Sacrament, I remember, the last time that you and I did.' This last fact, we should note, meant more in 1808 than it would now, for then the Sacrament was celebrated more rarely, so that to take it was a more conspicuous gesture of active devotion.

Jane Austen's religious convictions show themselves unexpectedly in one of her very few references to the public events of the day. In 1809, Sir John Moore was killed after triumphantly leading the English army on its retreat from Corunna. As he lay dying on the battlefield he whispered to his subordinate Colonel Hudson: 'You know I always wished to die like this. It is a great satisfaction to know that we have beaten the French – I hope the people of England will be satisfied.' The people of England were indeed satisfied; they also found Moore's last words moving and inspiring. Not so Jane Austen: she commented to Cassandra, 'I wish Sir John had united something of the Christian with the hero in his death.' Fervent patriot though she was, it yet jarred on her that any man in his last hours on earth, should be thinking of his country rather than of his God. Religious bias may account for another and curious reference she makes to Moore's death. On first hearing of it, she says to Cassandra that she was glad to learn that Moore's father was dead, since the loss of such a son must have been a great grief to him. Two days later, however, and after she had been told about his last words, she speaks in a disconcertingly different strain. 'I am sorry to find that Sir John Moore has a mother living; but, though a very heroic son, he might not be a very necessary one to her happiness.' Surely this is rather hard on poor Sir John; if his father had reason to mourn him, so also had his mother. Why did Jane Austen doubt it? A possible answer is that she had been so put off by what she considered his un-Christian last words as to doubt whether any mother could love such a son. A more likely explanation is that Jane Austen, profoundly anti-sentimental, had been irritated by the wave of emotion with which the public had reacted to the news of Moore's death and which may have included much sentimental sympathy for his mother. Neither explanation is very convincing. Both show her as for once a trifle unreasonable and captious.

This is particularly unexpected because, during the rest of her Southampton correspondence Jane Austen seems restored to her old equable self. She may not sparkle quite as brightly as in her twenties but she is equally observant, equally amused, equally and agreeably caustic. Sometimes she thought herself a little too caustic and felt guilty in consequence: 'I am forced to be abusive for want of subject, having really nothing to say,' she explains apologetically in one letter. Luckily for us, her sense of guilt did not unduly inhibit her, as the following passages demonstrate:

My Dearest Cassandra,

My expectation of having nothing to say to you after the conclusion of my last, seems nearer Truth than I thought it would be, for I feel to have but little. I need not therefore be above acknowledging the receipt of yours this morning; or of replying to every part of it which is capable of an answer; and you may accordingly prepare for my ringing the Changes of the Glads and Sorrys for the rest of the page. Unluckily however I see nothing to be glad of, unless I make it a matter of Joy that Mrs Wylmot has another son, and that Lord Lucan has taken a Mistress, both of which are of course joyful to the Actors.

Mrs Dundas seems a really agreeable woman – that is, her manners are gentle and she knows a great many of our connections in West Kent.

The death of Mrs W.K. we had seen; I had no idea that anybody liked her, but I am now feeling sorry on her husband's account and think that he had better marry Miss Sharp.

Lady Sondes's match surprises but does not offend me . . . I consider everybody as having a right to marry once in their lives for love, if they can; and, provided she will now leave off having bad headaches and being pathetic, I can allow her, I can wish her, to be happy.

Her aunt Mrs Leigh Perrot often gave her cause for amusement. 'She looks about with great diligence and success for inconvenience and evil – among which she ingeniously places the danger of her new housemaid catching cold on the outside of the coach when she goes down to Bath.' Now and again an individual case leads Jane Austen to make a generalization. On the institution of marriage for instance: detachedly and benevolently she recognizes its advantages.

> Your news of Edward Bridges was quite news [she writes on one occasion]. I wish him happy with all my heart and hope his choice may turn out according to his own expectations and beyond those of his family – I dare say it will. Marriage is a great improver . . . as to money that will come, you may be sure, because they cannot do without it.

But she thought that marriage involved obligations: Jane Austen, it seems, would not have sympathized with the modern and feminist view that wives are an oppressed race. She remarks of a discontented young wife of her acquaintance, 'As to pitying a young woman merely because she cannot live in two places at the same time and at once enjoy the comforts of being married and single, I would not attempt it.' For many people curiosity about their fellow humans is a thing of youth. Jane Austen's grew, if anything, with her advancing years and led her to be more and more surprised by them. Ironically she reflected on the unpredictability of human nature: 'Nobody,' she cries, 'ever feels or acts, suffers or enjoys as one expects!'

IV

Her relations and more especially her brothers continue to play a great part in her thoughts. In 1807 came the news that Charles, away at sea since 1805 and the one remaining bachelor in the family, had got married. His bride Fanny Palmer, daughter of the Attorney General at Bermuda, was a small pretty gentle girl of whom they were to grow very fond. But this was in the future; he was to be away from England for several years more. Not so his brothers: Frank, recently gone, was soon to be back in England for a time and Edward in Kent and Henry in London both lived close enough to see their mother and sisters at regular and not too distant intervals. James lived even closer and he and his wife came often to stay. This was not the pleasure that might have been expected. Mrs James Austen was the primary cause of trouble. She easily fancied herself slighted, was disagreeably unwilling to spend money and irritated her sisters-in-law by complaining about poverty, though in fact much better off than they were. They also thought her a bad influence on James, who was not always an easy guest.

> I am sorry and angry that his visits should not give one more pleasure [Jane writes to Cassandra]. The company of so good and so clever a man ought to be gratifying in itself; – but his chat seems all forced, his opinion on many points too much copied from his wife and his time here is spent I think in walking about the house and banging doors or ringing the bell for a glass of water.

Jane also complained to Cassandra about James's apparent indifference to Anna, his daughter by his first wife, and a particular favourite of her aunts. 'I have tried to give James pleasure by telling him of his daughter's taste but, if he felt, he did not express it.' These two passages contain the harshest words about a brother ever recorded of Jane Austen: they do suggest that he could be very trying, restlessly ringing the bell, bleakly unappreciative of a delightful daughter. All the same too much should not be made of Jane's remarks. Basically she was very fond of James. Within a year we find her affectionately praising him for his conscientiousness and unworldliness. Besides, the Austens' sense of the family bond was so strong, they felt such a sense of responsibility towards each other as to override any passing friction that might arise between individual members.

This family feeling was a great advantage to Jane and Cassandra; for it prevented them and their brothers drifting apart, even though they might live in different places. James often rode over from Steventon: and, if his visits were a mixed pleasure, they must at least have made a change. Edward came at regular intervals from Kent to see after his Hampshire property; this was close enough to Southampton to give him a chance to see his mother and sisters. His sisters also went to visit him at Godmersham. They usually stopped in London on the way to see Henry, now living in the Brompton district. Their visits to Godmersham lasted at least a month. Jane was there in the summer of 1808 and again in the spring of 1809. Staying at Godmersham was always an agreeable event. It was partly the setting: the big dignified mansion with its classic porch and spreading wings and, round it, stretches of turfy parkland, where the deer could be glimpsed grazing in the shadow of gracefully planted clumps of trees; and inside, a succession of elegant spacious rooms – Jane exclaims at the size of the Yellow Room which was her bedchamber in 1808 – where the guests' every comfort was attended to by one or other of the household servants; partly also the full and friendly social life, centred round dinner at the fashionable hour of six, with its courses enriched by French wines and made lively by the presence of a pack of children – Edward had

Godmersham Park, Kent: the seat of Edward (Austen) Knight

ten – and often some guests. All this was an exhilarating contrast to Jane's quiet home. On the other hand, it was not such a contrast as to make her feel out of place and ill at ease. Essentially, though on a greater scale, it was an example of the same mode of life as that she had been brought up to at Steventon Rectory, made up of the same elements, concerned with the same occupations. The gentlemen spent much of the day in sport or going to the races or riding round to inspect the estate; meanwhile the ladies walked in park and garden, embroidered, played on harp or piano, interested themselves in their children. The evenings were spent in cards or conversation or listening while Edward read aloud Walter Scott's newly published poem, 'Marmion'. The company too was composed of the same sort of people as at Steventon: members of the neighbouring country gentry, squires and clergymen and their wives and families and, nearly always, some Austen relations. In 1808 James and his family, as well as Jane, were staying at Godmersham. This mixture of homeliness and affluence, of the fresh and the familiar, suited Jane. Happily she spent her days observing her fellow guests, enjoying the beauties of the countryside, getting to know her young nephews and nieces.

This last activity made her 1808 visit especially memorable. She had always taken a particular interest in the children of her brothers. Now, on the verge of middle age and with less to interest her in her own fortunes, it grew stronger. She was curious to notice family traits appearing in a new generation. Moreover, interest in children went along with her general interest in human character. Children to her were not a race apart but responsible beings whose behaviour she watched in the same way as she watched that of her elders; noting for instance that James's son Edward played happily with his cousins while his sister, plain little Caroline, shrank from them in nervous shyness. This interest in children went along with a belief, typical of her period, in the paramount influence of upbringing on character. The eighteenth century, though it recognized the existence of inherited characteristics, never thought that they decided a man's destiny, for his will was free to modify them for good or ill. Which he opted for depended greatly on how he had been brought up. Jane Austen held this view strongly. It was to feature largely in her novels, and, in life, led her to look on children as potential adults and to treat them and their thoughts sympathetically and seriously. This seldom meant solemnly; there was never any question at any time of Jane Austen treating many things solemnly. Children enjoyed her company and she enjoyed theirs largely because they amused each other. She was equally at home with adolescents and as ready to enter into their thoughts and feelings. This capacity was the cause of an important event during this summer stay at Godmersham. Edward's daughter Fanny was now fifteen years old, pretty, dark-eyed, animated and enthusiastic. She and her Aunt Jane immediately took to each other. Fanny poured out her aspirations and hopes, Jane listened with amusement and growing affection. It was the start of a relationship that was later to mean a great deal to her. 'Almost another sister!' she exclaimed to Cassandra, 'I could not have supposed a niece would ever have been so much to me, she is quite after one's own heart.' It was the first time Jane had tasted the pleasures of friendship with someone of a younger generation. Partly for this reason, it was with regret that she said goodbye to Godmersham at the end of June. But regret was mixed with other feelings. Neither agreeable nieces nor excellent meals, nor spacious bedrooms could in the end make up for the absence of Cassandra and the intimate ease of intercourse with her. Just before leaving for Southampton, Jane wrote to her:

In another week I shall be at home; and then, my having been at Godmersham will seem like a Dream, as my visit to Brompton seems already. The Orange Wine will want our care soon. But in the meantime for elegance, ease and luxury; the Hattons and Milles dine her today and I shall eat ice and drink French wine, and be above vulgar economy. Luckily the pleasures of friendship, of unreserved conversation, of similarity of taste and opinions, will make good amends for Orange Wine.

In the autumn it was Cassandra's turn to go to Godmersham. Her visit was not to be so happy. Shortly after her arrival, Edward's wife Elizabeth gave birth to her eleventh child. She appeared to have survived her ordeal pretty well: then suddenly she took a turn for the worse: within a day or two she was dead. As always, the Austen family rallied round. Henry came down at once from London; Cassandra volunteered to stay for as long as she was wanted. Meanwhile Jane, at home with Mrs Austen, felt Elizabeth's death acutely. She had got to know the Godmersham family so well during the previous summer and could enter fully into their grief. All this appeared in the letters she wrote to Cassandra.

We have felt, we do feel, for you all – as you will not need to be told – for you, for Fanny, for Henry, for Lady Bridges, and for dearest Edward, whose loss and whose sufferings seem to make those of every other person nothing. God be praised! that you can say what you do of him – that he has a religious Mind to bear him up and a disposition that will gradually lead him to comfort. My dear, dear Fanny! I am so thankful that she has you with her! You will be everything to her, you will give her all the consolation that human aid can give. May the Almighty sustain you all – and keep you my dearest Cassandra well – but for the present I dare say you are equal to everything. . . . We need not enter into a Panegyric on the Departed – but it is sweet to think of her great worth – of her solid principles, her true devotion, her excellence in every relation of Life. It is also consolatory to reflect on the shortness of the sufferings which led her from this World to a better. Farewell for the present, my dearest Sister. Tell Edward that we feel for him and pray for him . . .

I suppose you see the corpse? How does it appear? We are anxious to be assured that Edward will not attend the funeral, but when it comes to the point, I think he must feel it impossible . . .

That you are for ever in our thoughts you will not doubt. I see your mournful party in my mind's eye under every varying circumstance of the day; and in the evening especially figure to myself its sad gloom: the efforts to talk, the frequent summons to melancholy orders and cares, and poor Edward restless in misery, going from one room to another, and perhaps not seldom upstairs, to see all that remains of his Elizabeth.

Like the letters she wrote after her father's death, these letters of Jane's present a strange mixture. They are thoroughly eighteenth-century in the formal rhetoric in which she expresses sentiments appropriate to such an occasion; also in her odd interest in the appearance of her late sister-in-law's corpse. But, mingled with these, is the vivid realism with which she imagines grief-stricken Godmersham and the figure of Edward pacing restlessly and aimlessly from one room to another. Jane longed to help Edward's family. She soon found occasion for it. Edward's sons, young Edward aged fourteen and George aged thirteen, happened to be visiting their Uncle James and his family at Steventon Rectory; now they came on to stay with their grand-mother and aunts at Southampton. Jane threw herself into the task of making their stay there as satisfactory as it could be in these tragic circumstances.

Edward and George came to us soon after seven on Saturday, very well but very cold, having by choice travelled on the outside, and with no great coat but what Mr Wise, the coachman, good-naturedly spared them of his, as they sat by his side. They were so much chilled when they arrived, that I was afraid they must have taken cold; but it does not seem at all the case; I never saw them looking better. They behave extremely well in every respect, showing quite as much feeling as one wishes to see, and on every occasion speaking of their father with the liveliest affection. His letter was read over by each of them yesterday, and with many tears; George sobbed aloud, Edward's tears do not flow so easily; but as far as I can judge they are both very properly impressed by what has happened. . . .

George is almost a new acquaintance to me, and I find him in a different way as engaging as Edward. We do not want amusement: bilbocatch, at which George is indefatigable, spillikins, paper ships, riddles, conundrums, and cards, with watching the flow and ebb of the river, and now and then a stroll out, keep us well employed. . . .

Mrs James Austen had not time to get them more than one suit of clothes; their others are making here, and although I do not believe Southampton is famous for tailoring, I hope it will prove itself better than Basingstoke. Edward has an old black coat, which will save his having a second new one; but I find that black pantaloons are considered by them as necessary, and of course one would not have them made uncomfortable by the want of what is usual on such occasions. . . .

I hope your sorrowing party were at church yesterday, and have no longer that to dread. Martha was kept at home by a cold, but I went with my two nephews and I saw Edward was much affected by the sermon, which, indeed, I could have supposed purposely addressed to the afflicted, if the text had not naturally come in the course of Dr Mant's observations on the Litany: 'All that are in danger, necessity, or tribulation,' was the subject of it. The weather did not allow us afterwards to get farther than the quay, where George was very happy as long as we could stay, flying about from one side to the other, and skipping on board a collier immediately.

In the evening we had the Psalms and Lessons, and a sermon at home, to which they were very attentive; but you will not expect to hear that they did not return to conundrums the moment it was over. Their aunt has written pleasantly of them, which was more than I had hoped.

While I write now, George is most industriously making and naming paper ships, at which he afterwards shoots with horse-chestnuts, brought from Steventon on purpose; and Edward equally intent over the 'Lake of Killarney' twisting himself about in one of our great chairs.

Jane Austen did not think that children can or should be shielded from tragedy; she approved of her nephews feeling their sorrows to the full and showing it. On the other hand she saw no reason to maintain an unchanging atmosphere of funeral gloom. Having given George and Edward the opportunity to pay their tribute of tears to their dead mother, she did all she could to cheer them up: and she was delighted if she succeeded. Indeed she was as good at getting on with schoolboys as with their sisters. How understandingly does she sympathize with their desire for conformity! If they thought it right to have black pantaloons as well as black coats, black pantaloons they should have.

We may note incidentally that Jane Austen did not expect her sister-in-law at Steventon to like Edward and George, let alone to enter into their feelings. She says to Cassandra with amusement 'their aunt has written pleasantly of them, which is more than I had hoped'. Her opinion of Mrs James Austen remained unenthusiastic.

V

Edward Austen's grateful affection for his mother and sisters now led him to concern himself about their future. He wanted to find them a home on his own property where he could see they were properly looked after. It is likely that with this end in view he offered them in the autumn of 1808 the choice of two houses, one on the Godmersham estate and one on his Hampshire property near Chawton Great House, a mansion of his, let for the next few years, but where, when the lease was up, he intended to spend part of his time. Mrs Austen and her daughters were delighted at the proposal; they had never settled down in Southampton. After consultation with the rest of the family, they decided on the Chawton house. Not surprisingly; it was in what they knew and loved as their native country and only a morning's ride from Steventon.

The next few months were spent in preparing for the move. Chawton Cottage, as their new house was named, would not be ready for them till the summer: but they proposed leaving Southampton in April, visiting friends and relations at Godmersham and elsewhere while they were waiting. Meanwhile Cassandra stayed on at Godmersham with Edward over Christmas. Until the end of January Jane's letters to her are mainly concerned with practical matters, together with giving the usual news of relations on land or at sea, scraps of local gossip, accounts of social life. There was more of this than usual at Southampton. Hearing that the Austens were leaving the place, neighbours called, and sent them invitations to goodbye gatherings. From curiosity and feelings of good will, Jane responded to these overtures. Together with Martha Lloyd, she also paid some last visits to the Southampton Theatre and attended balls in the Southampton Assembly Rooms.

A larger circle of acquaintance and an increase of amusement is quite in character with our approaching removal. Yes, I mean to go to as many Balls as possible, that I may have a good bargain. Everybody is very much concerned at our going away, and everybody is acquainted with Chawton and speaks of it as a remarkably pretty village; and everybody knows the House we describe – but nobody fixes on the right – I am very much obliged to Mrs Knight for such a proof of the interest she takes in me – and she may depend upon it, that I will marry Mr Papillon, whatever may be his reluctance or my own. – I owe her much more than such a trifling sacrifice. Our Ball was rather more amusing than I expected, Martha liked it very much, and I did not gape till the last quarter of an hour. It was the same room in which we danced 15 years ago! – I thought it all over – and, in spite of the shame of being so much older, felt with thankfulness that I was quite as happy now as then.

This passage stands out from other letters written at this time as stamped with a special significance. It indicates a landmark in Jane Austen's life. I do not know that these balls at Southampton were the last she ever went to; but they are the last she mentions in her letters, and perhaps, from now on, she made up

*Chawton Cottage. Drawing
by Anna Lefroy*

her mind that for her the time for balls was over. The time for marriage too: that she felt this is suggested by her smiling reference to Mrs Knight's idea of marrying her to Mr Papillon, the bachelor Rector of Chawton. It is as if in saying farewell to Southampton Jane Austen was also consciously saying farewell to her youth.

This might well have depressed her. She was facing a dull future as a spinster in reduced circumstances, confined indefinitely to a monotonous existence in a small country village. In fact, the letter shows her in excellent spirits. Looking round the Southampton Assembly Rooms and recalling the past, she even goes as far as to say that she is as happy as when she danced there as a girl of eighteen, fifteen years before. If she could have foreseen the years ahead, she would have been still happier. So far from confronting a dull prospect, she was about to enter a phase in her life story when, at last and triumphantly, her genius was to find fulfilment.

PART II

6

Life at Chawton

On 26 July 1809 just after her arrival at Chawton Jane Austen sent her brother Francis some light verses containing the following lines:

> As for ourselves, we're very well
> As unaffected prose will tell –.
> Cassandra's pen will paint our state
> The many comforts that await
> Our Chawton home, how much we find
> Already in it, to our mind;
> And how convinced, that when complete
> It will all other Houses beat
> That ever have been made or mended
> With rooms concise, or rooms distended.

In these lines, Jane Austen seems to be following her professed principle of making the reasonable best of things. Compared with most modern dwellings, Chawton Cottage is a pleasant place – what Georgian house is not? – but it is unlikely that she really thought that, even when finished, 'it would all other Houses beat'. A plain two-storied unpretentious building of russet brick, with sash windows and tiled roof, it faced immediately on the village street near the corner where the road from Gosport joined the highroad from London to Winchester. Its front opened on a combined hall and dining room: on the left of this was a sitting room looking out on the garden. Behind were the kitchen and other offices; upstairs, a narrow passage opened on five bedrooms. All the rooms, above and below, were on the small side, with low

Chawton House and Church. Oil painting, 1809

ceilings and, except for a prettily moulded mantelpiece in the sitting room, not much attempt in them at decoration. At the back of the house were some outbuildings; a bakehouse and stable where the Austen ladies were later to keep a donkey and cart. Surrounding the whole was a large garden, part flower, part vegetable, part turfy orchard. Round this ran a thickly planted shrubbery walk, in the shelter of which the Austens and Martha Lloyd liked to take the air and a little mild exercise. 'You cannot imagine – it is impossible to imagine – what nice walks we have round the orchard!' remarked Jane. The shrubbery, like the Southampton garden, had a syringa in it to suggest memories of Cowper; beneath it bloomed a border gay in Maytime with pinks and sweet williams and columbines. The garden was screened on one side from the Winchester road by a high hedge of hornbeam planted by Edward Austen to make it quieter and more private. For the same reason, he now walled up a window of the sitting room looking on the road and made another in the wall that opened on the green tranquillity of the garden. Meanwhile anyone who wanted a more lively view could, from the window of the hall-dining room, get a glimpse of the stir of the great world as manifested in the ever varying traffic of the highroad: coaches and carriages, farm carts and curricles, trotting horsemen and trudging pedestrians, farmers spanking along in their gigs, naval officers on leave cantering up for a spree in the capital and, four or five times in the year, the boys of Winchester School arriving for term or dispersing for the holidays. During pauses in the rattle of the long distance traffic, the scene was gently animated by the dawdling movement of village life.

> Emma went to the door for her amusement [so runs a passage in Jane Austen's novel *Emma*] . . . and when her eyes fell only on the butcher with his tray, a tidy old woman travelling homewards from shop with her full basket, two curs quarrelling over a dirty bone, and a string of dawdling children round the baker's little bow-window eyeing the gingerbread, she knew she had no reason to complain, and was amused enough; quite enough still to stand at the door. A mind lively and at ease, can do with seeing nothing, and can see nothing that does not answer.

Jane Austen's was such a mind; for Emma we may read the name of her creator, looking out from the hall window of Chawton Cottage and finding herself 'amused enough'. Though no architectural masterpiece, both by its

The Great House and Park at Chawton. Gouache

situation and its modest pleasant rooms, it suggested security and peace. Yet it was sufficiently linked with the outside world to prevent its inhabitants feeling isolated and cut off. Even if her praise of it is exaggerated, Jane Austen had good reason to like it.

This was lucky for she was to spend the rest of her days there. Very quiet days too; her earlier life cannot be described as crowded with incident; but it was not wholly uneventful. In it, she had grown up, made friends and been bereaved of them, had fallen in love and been disappointed of love's fulfilment, had been sought in marriage, lost her father and, more than once, changed her home. Now and until the day of her death, her place and mode of living were to be unchanged and her personal life almost without incident. Indeed her establishment at Chawton marks the turning point in her story. Nothing more was to happen to Jane Austen the woman: from now on her history is that of Jane Austen the artist.

Map of Hampshire showing Chawton

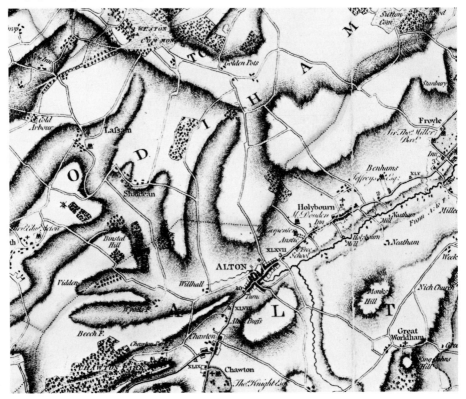

Only her close relations were to realize this. She herself was always to keep quiet about her literary activities. To most people she continued to be thought just another unmarried country lady and living the life expected of such a person. Jane Austen accepted this role; indeed she actively entered into it. More than necessary, thought her younger relations. She had not yet lost her youthful charm of looks, her light figure and bright eyes and clear olive skin; one of her nieces remembered her as the first person who ever struck her as pretty. But she deliberately dressed in the style of an older woman, no longer went in for keeping up with the fashions and generally wore a cap, one of the badges of middle age. Cassandra did likewise. In the past both sisters had been thought noticeably well-dressed. Now the best that could be said of their clothes was that they were clean and neat. In both, this was a sign that they had given up all thought of marriage: also of an active social life. This was partly inevitable. There was no theatre or assembly rooms near Chawton; while to take much part in the diversions of county society – dinner parties, card parties, garden parties – involved keeping a carriage. The Austens could not afford a carriage: they had to be content with such company as was within walking distance. In this company they found no one with whom they had enough in common to become an intimate friend. At Chawton the Austen ladies and Martha Lloyd kept themselves to themselves.

II

They did not however find their lives dull or empty. For one thing they had the house to run. Mrs Austen had given this over to her daughters: it bored her. She preferred to spend her time at her embroidery or, when the weather was fine enough, working in the garden, especially the kitchen garden. Though over seventy, she was still vigorous and could often be seen from the window, dressed in a labourer's round green smock, digging energetically in a potato patch. Though the Austens kept a maid for indoor and a man for outdoor and garden work, these were both simple untrained rustics and their employers had a lot to do supervising and helping them. They also did housework themselves. The result was a credit to them. Visitors exclaimed at how well-kept Chawton Cottage was, how comfortable and welcoming! Cassandra, as the elder, was in official command of housekeeping operations; but, if she went away, Jane understood them well enough to take over without difficulty and with some pleasure. Catering seems to have interested her; she enjoyed her food. 'Good apple pies are a considerable part of our domestic happiness', she comments on one occasion. Even when Cassandra was at home, some things were left to Jane's care. She had charge of the sugar and tea and of their modest cellar, composed mostly of spruce beer and home-made wines. It was Jane too who made breakfast.

Her day started earlier than this. Before breakfast was her time for practis-ing on a piano bought for £30 and now installed in the sitting room. She practised early in order not to inconvenience the others, who were none of them musical. She herself was only moderately so, judged by any stringent standard. Perhaps she played as well as Emma Woodhouse, but not so well as Jane Fairfax; and I doubt that she could have performed a 'powerful concerto' with the skill reported of Marianne Dashwood. Nor would she have much enjoyed listening to someone else doing so. Her musical taste seems to have been on the lowbrow side. We have some of her music copied out in her own hand: none of it suggests that she knew she was living in the greatest of musical periods and was the contemporary of Haydn and Mozart. On the other hand she was particularly fond of two songs called 'The Soldier's Lament' and 'The Yellow Haired Laddie'. Moreover the conversation of enthusiastic music lovers could fill her with amused dismay. 'I have been listening to dreadful insanity,' she wrote once, 'it is Mr H's firm belief that a person not musical is fit for every sort of wickedness. I ventured to assert a little on the other side but

(left) Title-page to one of Jane Austen's music books
(right) Title-page to a music book belonging to the Austen family

Mrs George Austen
(1739–1827)

wished the cause in abler hands.' After listening to what struck her as such extravagant ravings, Jane Austen felt herself drawn to a Miss Holder simply because she owned that she had no taste for music. All the same Jane's liking for it was genuine so far as it went. Her nephew Edward was to remember her playing and singing traditional songs with spirit and sweetness. Anyway, if she did not enjoy music at all, why did she bother to get up early in order to practise?

After breakfast, she spent the morning reading and writing on a small mahogany desk in the combined hall and dining room; the drawing room presumably was occupied by the other ladies. At midday came luncheon or 'Noonshine' as Jane sometimes called it, a light snack of a meal. After lunch was the time for going out: a stroll round the shrubbery walk, if she was tired or the weather not good, but generally further afield. Sometimes she went shopping in the little market town of Alton about a mile away, sometimes indulged her taste for the charms of nature by taking a walk through the leafy or leafless Hampshire lanes or amid the magnificent beechwoods of Chawton Park or on the turfy lawns around Chawton Great House, a Jacobean mansion, part grey stone, part red brick, whose gates stood just down the road beyond the village. Dinner, the chief meal of the day, was early, between three and half past four. Afterwards the ladies settled down for the evening, occupying themselves sometimes with sewing or cards, but always with conversation. It seldom seems to have been solemn conversation; for it is described by her nephews and nieces as very amusing and punctuated by fits of laughter. Jane also liked for a change to play some game demanding skill of hand, like spillikins or Cup and Ball. No one it was said could throw spillikins in more perfect a circle; and she had been known to catch the ball in the cup one hundred times in succession, only giving up when she was too tired to go on. Finally, as usual, the Austens spent many evenings reading aloud. Here Jane showed she possessed the family talent for acting. When reading from Fanny Burney's *Evelina* she impersonated the heroine's vulgar relations so vividly that listening to her gave the same kind of pleasure as going to a well-acted play.

She also read a good deal to herself; old favourites like Richardson's novels or Cowper's poems, and also any new books she could get hold of. She much admired Maria Edgeworth's novels but could get pleasure out of biographies and travel books and history books. Poetry she read less, to judge from the references to it in her letters, though she did enjoy Walter Scott's verse tales and also, if her taste was like that of her heroine Anne Elliot's, some of Byron's. But the tone in which she speaks of these last suggests that Byronic emotion, especially Byronic despair, appealed to her as little as one would expect. Very different was her reaction to the poems of Crabbe. Some of these had appeared more than twenty years before: but I imagine, it was during her Chawton years and after the publication of his masterpieces, 'The Borough' and 'The Tales', that she got to know his work well. The result was that he joined Cowper and Johnson as one of her three favourite authors. This is not surprising. His shrewd eye for character, his gift for story-telling, the vivid detailed accuracy with which he portrays the less obviously picturesque kind of English landscape, were all things likely to please her. Moreover – given the difference between his melancholy and her serene temperament – his view of life had much in common with hers: moral, unsentimental, realistic and rooted deep in the same strong, sober Anglican faith. Not only did she admire him as a great writer, she also felt him a kindred soul and took trouble to find out all she could about his life and character. She would have liked to have been Mrs Crabbe, she said: and when she heard that his wife had died, 'Poor woman!' she wrote gaily to Cassandra, 'I will comfort him as well as I can, but I do not undertake to be good to his children. She had better not have any!'

III

True life stories interested her as much and more as those she found in books. Cassandra, a more executive type than her sister, did a certain amount of charitable work in the village: as well as making clothes for the poor, she visited the cottages where she heard there were people in want, taught girls to

Crabbe   1826

The Reverend George Crabbe

sew and read and heard them their Catechism. Jane now and again helped with the reading lessons, but otherwise did not take part in these doings. But she was interested to hear the accounts of the drama and comedy of village life that Cassandra brought back with her. Any story about the life of their neighbours in village or county stirred her interest, and, if possible, her amusement. This did not mean however that she much wanted to meet the persons involved. In the same way as she accepted the costume of middle age, Jane Austen readily accepted the fact that circumstances now cut her off from a full social life. She could even seem unwilling to take part in it. This sometimes created an unfavourable impression.

> A friend of mine [so runs an account of her written during these later years] says that she has stiffened into the most perpendicular, precise taciturn piece of single blessedness that ever existed . . . no more regarded in society than a poker or a fire screen or any other thin, upright piece of wood or iron that fills the corner in peace and quietness.

This description has for its author Miss Mitford, not, as we have seen, a reliable witness about Jane Austen. For all her professional admiration for her writings, she is suspiciously ready to believe any hard words about the private character of her distinguished fellow author. To describe Jane Austen in her thirties as a thin upright piece of wood must surely have been as much a misrepresentation as it had been to describe the girl Jane Austen as a husband-hunting butterfly. But, in the same way, it may well have been the exaggeration of a truth. Can it be that Jane Austen had never completely got over the shyness in company which had afflicted her as a child and that the apparent social confidence, which she had acquired when she first grew up, was a superficial affair that had begun to dwindle with the dwindling of youthful spirits? It is possible too that settling down to an uneventful future, her interest in the human comedy grew less that of one taking part in it and more and more that of a detached novelist observer. If she happened to find herself among strangers, here was another reason for her to sit back and be silent.

But only when she was among strangers: and this did not mean just when she was alone with her mother and Cassandra and Martha Lloyd. Chawton Cottage was, in its modest way, a family centre with the Austen brothers and their families coming and going and sometimes leaving a child behind for a longer stay. Nor was home confined to Chawton. Jane and Cassandra made an occasional leisurely visit to Henry in London or Edward at Godmersham; and the strength of the Austen family bond was such as to make the house of any one of them a home to the others. Now that Jane was older and poorer, her social life was mainly provided for by her brothers: but, since these brothers were affectionate and hospitable and had, most of them, families of their own, she was not cut off from society. Moreover it was the society that she liked best. The Austens had always enjoyed each other's company more than that of anyone else and they continued to do so. Time and separation did not weaken their love for each other: in the case of the sisters, it had

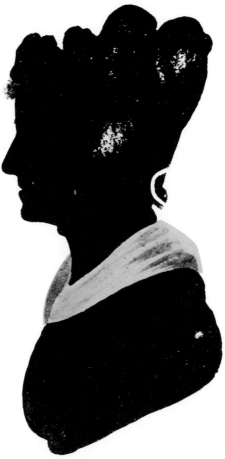

Cassandra Austen (1773–1845), Jane's elder sister

strengthened it. For, since neither had married, their capacity of affection had not been diverted to new objects but had come to concentrate itself on their brothers and their families. Jane remained a devoted sister. In the same verses that she had written to Frank on her first arrival at Chawton, she congratulated him on the birth of his son and declared her love and admiration for him himself.

My dearest Frank, I wish you joy
Of Mary's safety with a Boy,
Whose birth has given little pain
Compared with that of Mary Jane. —
May he a growing Blessing prove,
And well deserve his Parents' Love! —
Endow'd with Art's & Nature's Good,
Thy name possessing with thy Blood,
In him, in all his ways, may we
Another Francis William see! —
Thy infant days may he inherit,
Thy warmth, nay insolence of spirit; —
We would not with one fault dispense
To weaken the resemblance.
  May he revive thy Nursery sin,
Peeping as daringly within,
His curley Locks but just descried,
With "Bet, my be not come to bide." —
    Fearless of danger, braving pain,
  And threaten'd very oft in vain,
    Still may one Terror daunt his soul,
    One needful engine of Controul

A poem written by Jane Austen to her brother Frank on the birth of his son

My dearest Frank, I wish you joy
Of Mary's safety with a boy,
Whose birth has given little pain
Compared with that of Mary Jane.
May he on growing blessing prove
And well deserve his Parents' love!
Endowed with Art's and Nature's Good,
Thy name possessing with thy Blood,
In him, in all his ways, may we
Another Francis William see!
Thy infant days may be inherit
Thy warmth, nay insolence of spirit
We would not with one fault dispense
To weaken the resemblance . . .
So may his equal faults as Child,
Produce Maturity as mild!
His Saucy words and fiery ways
In early Childhood's pettish days.
In Manhood, shew his Father's mind
Like him, considerate and kind;
All gentleness to those around
And eager only not to wound.

Her family returned her affection and enjoyed her society. For them, there was no question of her sitting back shy and silent. No one at Chawton or Godmersham thought of comparing Jane Austen to a poker or a fire screen: with her relations she talked easily and delightfully. They looked forward to her coming and missed her when she was gone. This was as true of the younger generation as of their elders. She had always responded to their appreciation. Her interest and pleasure in young people grew stronger than before: the last important relationships she was ever to form were those with her nephews and nieces. Not of course with all of them: there were too many. By the time Jane Austen died her brother James had three children, Frank five, Charles three and Edward no less than eleven. No one could be intimate with all of these. But Jane took some note of most and some she got to know very well. Of these, James's family lived close by; Edward's she met at Godmersham or later at Chawton Great House and his boys on their way to and from school at Winchester; Charles's three daughters were more than once deposited by their parents for a lengthy stay at Chawton.

There they were Jane's especial care and responsibility: for once it was she and not Cassandra who took the lead. The children preferred it that way. This worried Jane, who continued to regard her sister as a much superior being to herself. From time to time she felt herself bound to explain to a child that she or he had much better go to Aunt Cassandra for advice and help as Aunt Cassandra knew much more than Aunt Jane did and could impart her knowledge much better. The child listened silent but unconvinced. For all of them Jane remained easily their favourite aunt and they liked staying at Chawton because she was there.

> Her charm to children [wrote James's daughter Caroline] was great sweetness of manner and she seemed to love you, and you loved her naturally in return. This as well as I can now recollect and analyse, was what I felt in my earliest days, before I was old enough to be amused by her cleverness; but soon came the delight of her playful talk. Everything she could make amusing to a child. Then, as I got older, and when cousins came to share the entertainment, she would tell us the most delightful stories chiefly of Fairyland, and her Fairies had all characters of their own. The tale was invented, I am sure, at the moment, and was sometimes continued for two or three days, if occasion served.
>
> When staying at Chawton, if my two cousins Mary Jane and Cassy were there, we often had amusements in which my Aunt was very helpful. She was the one to whom we always looked for help. She would furnish us with what we wanted from her wardrobe, and she would often be the entertaining visitor in our make-believe house. She amused us in various ways and once, I re-member, in giving a conversation as between myself and my two cousins, supposed to be grown-up, the day after the Ball.

From Caroline's words, it is clear that Jane Austen enjoyed the company of children, partly because it gave her a chance to gratify her taste and talent for nonsense and comic fantasy. This was very strong; it had shown itself exub-erantly in her early skits and sketches. But she had found little outlet for it since: her own novels were of their nature confined to the realm of reality. This did not mean however that she had lost her taste for fantasy: and she was able to find fulfilment for it in the tales she told the children. It appeared at its most extreme and nonsensical in her tales for little children; but it showed itself in a modified form in her talk to their older brothers and sisters. Though careful to keep her more caustic jokes for the ears of Cassandra alone, Jane Austen got and gave a great deal of fun by inventing openly preposterous stories about her neighbours, especially the neighbours she hardly knew; and then retailing them, adding detail to fantastic detail as her imagination took fire, and sometimes going on to write them down in prose or verse. 'As an instance,' writes Caroline, 'I would give her description of the pursuits of Miss Mills and Miss Yates – two young ladies of whom she knew next to nothing – they were only on a visit to a near neighbour but their names tempted her into rhyme and on she went!'

'I have always maintained the importance of Aunts,' Jane Austen once remarked; and indeed she was born to be one. On the one hand she had an unusual taste and turn for getting on with young people, on the other her strong family feeling drew her naturally to those young people who were also her relations. It may be too that her nephews and nieces took the place for her of the children she might have had. Normal and feminine as she was in so many ways, it is unlikely that Jane Austen was without some maternal instinct. But it was not a very strong one; no more than could be fully satisfied in the role of an aunt. There was a reason for this and she knew it. She did not need children to make her happy, she used to say. She added, 'My books are my children.'

Uttered playfully, this remark is crucially revealing. It gives us the master key to the understanding of Jane Austen's character and life story. For most of her life the two strains in her had worked harmoniously together. It was her life as a woman that provided her with the particular material needed to inspire her art; yet it never so much absorbed her as for long to interfere with the functioning of her life as an artist. However wholeheartedly she seemed as a woman to enter into the life around her, into its joys and sorrows and pleasures and problems, Jane Austen the artist was present at them, a detached invisible figure, observant to gather the fuel that might one day kindle her imaginative spark to flame. Here it was that she differed from most women. The creative impulse which in them fulfilled itself as wife and mother in her fulfilled itself as an artist. Gradually, and influenced by chance and circumstances, this became more and more apparent: more and more the artist in her began to dominate and at last took over to become the centre and motive force of her existence.

Her establishment at Chawton marks this central turning point in her story. Life there, apparently so stagnant, served rather to provide the needed time and incentive for her genius to operate. Her circumstances were liberating, not frustrating. With her future secure and leisurely and any idea of marriage dismissed from her mind, she was at last completely free to concentrate on her art. There is evidence that she had begun to do so before leaving Southampton. In April 1809 she wrote to Crosby the publisher, asking him to send back the manuscript of *Susan* – later *Northanger Abbey* – if he did not mean to publish it: and some months before she had lent a story she had written to her niece Fanny to see what she thought of it. Now, established at Chawton, she settled down to spend the rest of her life as a dedicated author.

IV

It remained a secret dedication. Even more than before, if possible: Jane Austen's obsessive secrecy about her writing is the nearest thing to an eccentricity in her otherwise well-balanced character. She even tried to conceal her real name from her publisher; in her letter to Crosby she called herself Mrs Ashton Dennis. Meanwhile, at Chawton and elsewhere, her double life went on. Her neighbours knew her only as the daughter of a late rector of Steventon and at home nobody was aware of her literary work except her closest relations and Martha Lloyd. She took elaborate pains to conceal it from anyone else: friends, visitors, servants. This is all the more significant because it was not easy. She had no private room to write in, except the small bedroom she shared with Cassandra. Leaving the sitting room to the other ladies, she chose to work in the combined front hall and dining room at a little table on which she had placed her mahogany desk. She wrote on small pieces of paper because this made it easier for her, if interrupted, to slip them into a drawer or under a blotter. The room led, by way of a swing door, to the kitchen and other offices. Though this door creaked disagreeably, Jane Austen asked that it should be allowed to go on doing so. Her unspoken reason was that the creak gave her warning that someone was coming, so that she had time to hide her manuscript before he or she entered. In later years, she seems to have relaxed her vigilance sufficiently to do some of her writing in the general sitting room, whether at home or staying with one of her brothers. Another of her nieces, Edward's daughter Marianne, remembers her sitting sewing by the fire of a winter's evening. Suddenly she would burst out laughing, jump up, run across to the writing table and scribble down a sentence there; then, without explanation, she would come back and resume her seat by the fire.

7

Fulfilment

Jane Austen found herself as an author extremely young. But for many years her gifts were frustrated of complete fulfilment. She could not find a publisher for her first books and, after that, personal and family troubles combined with no settled home to get between her and sustained literary effort. She was thirty-four years old before she sat down at her mahogany desk in the dining room at Chawton Cottage to get finally and fully started on a literary career. Once started, she did not stop. During the next seven and a half years she completed six novels and began a seventh.

As it turned out, delay and frustration proved to have been to her advantage, for it had given her art time and opportunity to ripen. On the one hand, it had enabled her to acquire a deeper and wider acquaintance with human character: on the other, from her own experience and the study of other people's books, she had learned a more expert mastery of her craft; with the result that, when they did appear, her books were all the product of her maturity. It is true that three of them – *Sense and Sensibility*, *Pride and Prejudice*, *Northanger Abbey* – were new versions of earlier drafts: and their tone has a touch of spirited youthfulness that distinguishes them from their successors. But, before she allowed them to be seen by the public, Jane Austen revised them extensively in the light of her riper judgment; so that in fact both in accomplishment and in the view of life they present, they are mature works. Moreover her later novels – *Mansfield Park, Emma* and *Persuasion* – though written after 1809, were also the fruits of her past in that they must have been drawn from experience acquired before settling at Chawton. Jane Austen never repeated herself and each of her books is distinguished from the others by important individual differences. But, allowing for this, the six may be taken together as the homogeneous and perfected expression of her genius, for which all her preceding thirty-four years had been prelude and preparation.

It seems then an appropriate moment for anyone aspiring to paint her portrait to pause and examine the character of that genius; and to consider its relation to her personality and life story. It was a genius for a particular kind of novel-writing. In *Northanger Abbey*, she praises the novels she admired most as displaying 'thorough knowledge of human nature, the happiest delineation of its varieties, the liveliest effusions of wit and humour, conveyed to the world in the best chosen language': and these, though not the outstanding characteristics of all the world's great novels, are very much those of the sort Jane Austen aspired to write. Her efforts to do so were conditioned by two factors. Her view of human nature was limited in the first place by her circumstances: she wrote about men and women as she herself had known them. Her view was further limited by her sex, by the fact that she only saw as much of humanity as was visible to a lady, and this when a lady's view was narrowly confined by convention, so that the only people she ever knew well belonged to her class and lived in her neighbourhood. Secondly – and this is more important – her view was conditioned by the nature of her inspiration. It was confined to those aspects of human nature which happened to stimulate her individual creative imagination. For Jane Austen, this meant life in its private aspects; she was stirred to portray men and women only in relation to their family and friends and social acquaintances. Further, she looked at these mainly through the eyes of a comedian. Her first efforts at writing as a schoolgirl had been designed to make herself and her readers laugh; and to the end of her days humour was an integral part of her creative process. As her imagination started to function, a smile began to spread itself across her face: nor did it ever leave it for long. The smile is the signature on the finished work. It is the angle of her humorous vision, the light of her ironic amusement that gives its distinctive sparkle and perspective to her picture of the world. To sum up, Jane Austen's work can be described as a realistic picture of social and domestic life, seen from a woman's point of view and treated in a spirit of comedy.

Such a picture obviously leaves much out: on the one hand the solemn and the tragic, on the other, all that is neither domestic nor personal. Jane Austen recognized the limitations within which she should work. She was aware that hers was a comedy talent. It was once suggested to her that she should write an historical romance. Gaily and unhesitatingly she refused:

> I could no more write a romance than an epic poem. I could not sit seriously down to write a serious romance under any other motive than to save my life; and if it were indispensable for me to keep it up and never relax into laughing at myself or at other people, I am sure I should be hung before I had finished the first chapter.

Equally she knew she should write only about worlds of which she herself had experience. She was happy it should be so: 'Two or three families in a country village is the very thing to work on,' she said. She also realized that to portray so familiar a scene convincingly meant taking care to be factually correct down to the smallest detail. 'Are there hedges in Northampton?' she asks a correspondent, when she was writing *Mansfield Park* which was set in that county: and to her niece Anna, engaged on a first novel, she wrote: 'Do not set your story in Ireland if you have not been there. You will be in danger of giving false representations.' Probability she thought as important as accuracy. It does not sound natural, she told Anna, to represent a lover as addressing his beloved in the third person; nor should she describe a man as going for a walk the day after he had broken his arm, even if she knew somebody who had done so: 'It is so little usual as to appear unnatural in a book.'

She put her principles into practice. Especially was she careful to stay within the limits imposed by her circumstances and the nature of her talent. After the unsuccessful experiment of *Lady Susan*, she never strays from the world she herself had lived in; and, though her heroines may go on a visit to Bath or London, their home is always in the country. Her characters all come from her own class; nor does she trespass beyond the boundaries set by her sex. She never describes a scene at which no woman was present: her heroes are shown fragmentarily and with character and motives in part unexplained, as they appeared to the girls with whom they came in contact. In the same way, she stays within the area determined by the nature of her genius. All her stories are stories of private life and turn on personal relationships: between parents and children, brothers and sisters, between a man and woman in love. Critics like to point out that, though she lived during the period of the French Revolution and the Napoleonic Wars, these never appear in her books. As we have seen, this was not because she was unaware of them: her cousin by marriage had been guillotined and she had two brothers, whom she deeply loved, fighting in the wars. But neither revolution nor war inspired the artist in her: they play no part in private and domestic life. Nor were they material for her type of comedy. She excludes from her scenes any subject matter that, for one reason or another, is incompatible with the comic spirit. All her plots had happy endings; there are no deaths in them or scenes of crime or vice. At the close of *Mansfield Park*, it is true, serious sin does show signs of intruding itself in the shape of Maria Rushworth's adulterous elopement with Henry Crawford. Jane Austen however does not permit these sinners to appear on the stage in person; and, after two or three pages, dismisses them and their doings from the scene in two firm sentences. 'Let other pens dwell on guilt and misery,' she writes, 'I quit such odious subjects as soon as I can.' She realized that any adequate treatment of these subjects would jar with the cool comedy mood which pervades the rest of the book. Rightly therefore, she avoided them.

She avoided jarring characters too. A large number of her *dramatis personae* are comic character parts put in purposely to make the reader laugh: and even those characters with whom she is in sympathy – even her heroines – are, most of them, touched with the comic spirit, people to be laughed with and sometimes to be laughed at. Only once does she try another type, Fanny Price in *Mansfield Park*: and for many readers – I am one of them – she is not a complete success. She is convincingly real; we believe in her virtues, her unselfishness and conscientiousness. But she never laughs, at herself nor at anyone else; and her creator – perhaps because she is trying sympathetically to draw someone very unlike herself – hesitates to do more than now and again smile gently at her. Her comic spirit is subdued by her tenderness towards 'My Fanny', as she calls her; with the result that Fanny does seem a little priggish and spiritless. All the more because the charm that should have compensated for her lack of humour – her innocent sweetness, the romantic sensibility that made her appreciate Cowper's poetry and the green groves of Southerton – are things that cannot effectively be conveyed in a comedy vein; so that, though Jane Austen mentions them, she fails to make us respond to them. We realize her limitations because for once she has trespassed beyond them.

Romantic feelings were always a problem to Jane Austen the novelist; and not just because she found it so easy to laugh at them. To do justice to those involved the expression of direct emotion and, as we know from her letters and poems, natural shyness together with an Austen upbringing hampered her ability to express emotion directly. In life she liked and approved of people with warm spontaneous feelings – this is clear both from her novels and her letters – but, herself, she found it difficult to put such feelings into words. When the plot of a story required her to do so, the result is all too often stiff and even absurd: 'The evergreen,' exclaims Fanny Price rhapsodizing on the beauties of nature as exhibited in the Mansfield shrubberies, 'how beautiful, how wonderful, how welcome the evergreen!' These are not the right words with which to persuade the reader to enter into Fanny's woodland raptures. Such lapses, however, are luckily rare; for in general Jane Austen took care to avoid the occasion for them. Her stories are all love stories: but we only hear one of her lovers, the self-controlled Mr Knightley, declare his love. Movingly does Jane Austen convey the consuming passion of Marianne Dashwood but she does it mainly by implication, by showing how it colours her moods and reveals itself in her actions, not by her actual words. Only in her last novel, and then very restrainedly, has Jane Austen learned to express emotion in words that are themselves eloquent and poignant.

There have been few artists indeed with such a clear idea as Jane Austen had of what they could do and what they could not. Two memorable remarks from her letters illustrate her awareness. To her nephew Edward she described her work, with humorous self-depreciation, as 'that little bit (two inches wide) of ivory, in which I work with so fine a brush as produces little effect after much labour'; and she rejects the suggestion that she should write an historical romance with a categorical pronouncement: 'No, I must keep to my own style, go on in my own way; and, though I may never succeed in that, I am convinced that I should totally fail in any other.'

She had no reason to worry; keeping to her own style, she triumphed. Jane Austen was rewarded for her self-knowledge and self-restraint. There is hardly an inch of her picture of the human scene that has not been checked by reference to reality and passed through the transfiguring medium of her creative vision. The consequence is that its whole surface vibrates with life and individuality. No wonder that readers still find her books enjoyable! But they are something more: they are also impressive, penetrating, deeply interesting. For her genius was twofold. Along with her comedy sense she possessed a subtle insight into the moral nature of man. The union of the two is the distinguishing characteristic of her achievement; and it makes these lively unpretentious comedies of social and domestic life the vehicle of profound and illuminating comments on the human drama. This shows most obviously in her power to create characters that are, in the fullest sense, living. It does not matter that she shows them to us mainly in a comedy context. In its own cooler, more detached spirit, great comedy deals with fundamental and unchanging elements in human character just as much as does tragedy. Jane Austen's comedy is of this kind. It does not matter either that she draws people only in their private aspect. A man's essential nature reveals itself just as much in relation to his family as in relation to his professional career or his in- tellectual convictions. Perhaps more; if you want to know about a man's gifts, you should see him at work, if you want to know about his temper, you should see him at home. Nor is Jane Austen's view rendered less penetrating by the fact that, as a rule, she shows him not in moments of crisis but in the trivial incidents of every day. Human nature discloses itself as fully in little things as in big ones: a tea party reveals selfishness, kindness, self-control, ill temper, as much as does an air raid. Only you must have the faculty to discern them. Jane Austen had. She had a sharp eye for the surface qualities of personality, people's manner and demeanour and tricks of speech. But she could also discern the hidden structure that lay beneath the surface; her mind was always at work to discover the principles of action that determined her subject's conduct, the particular combination of qualities and weaknesses that went to compose his or her individuality: she shows these surface peculiarities in relation to these concealed and determining factors. In consequence she does not need to present her characters as involved in catastrophes that would be out of place in a comedy. On the very few occasions when her plot requires her to do so, she rises to the occasion admirably. When Louisa Musgrove falls, apparently lifeless, on the Cobb at Lyme, Jane Austen describes convincingly the different ways the various characters react to what appears to be a disastrous situation. But, though we admire her insight, it tells us nothing new about these people; the uneventful walks and evening parties where we have already seen them have revealed their disposition so fully that we could have foretold how they would behave.

Indeed Jane Austen's understanding of the moral nature of man is, within the limits of her experience, complete. However slight its manifestation, however muffled by convention or disguised by personal charm, unfailingly she detects the essential quality of character. The Miss Bertrams:

> . . . joined to beauty and brilliant acquirements a manner naturally easy, and carefully formed to general civility and obligingness. . . . Their vanity was in such good order, that they seemed to be quite free from it, and gave themselves no airs, while the praises attending such behaviour . . . served to strengthen them in believing they had no faults.

Only two sentences; but we understand the Miss Bertrams completely.

All the more so because we can trust their creator to be fair to them. Jane Austen's concern for truth and the consistent irony of her attitude make her wonderfully impartial. Her most high-principled characters have their weakness: Edmund Bertram allows his infatuation with Mary Crawford to blind him to her faults against his better judgment; Jane Bennet's determination to see good in everyone leads her to deceive herself to the point of absurdity. Jane Austen is equally fair to her disagreeable characters. Mrs Norris is odious, far more so than her sister, silly, harmless Mrs Price; but Jane Austen also points out that the same meddling energy which made her so unpleasant would have fitted her far better than Mrs Price to cope with the difficulties of an impecunious sailor's wife with a large family. Again, she notes the fact that Bingley's sisters were false and snobbish did not stop them from being agreeable company, 'able to relate an anecdote with humour and laugh at an acquaintance with spirit'. This impartiality gives her characters volume: they are solid, three-dimensional figures that can be looked at from several sides.

So searching an insight into character gives Jane Austen's portraits a timeless quality. They are universal types. Miss Bates is the type of all bores, John

Thorpe is the type of all brainless bumptious young men, his sister Isabella the type of all gushing calculating flirts, Mary Musgrove the type of all self-pitying discontented wives. When Mr Woodhouse tells us that his grandchildren are 'all remarkably clever, they will come and stand by my chair and say Grandpa can you give us a bit of string?', he voices the fatuous fondness of all doting grandparents. When Darcy says, 'I have been selfish all my life in practice, not in principle', he confesses the besetting weakness of all men who, though conscientious and unegotistic are accustomed to have their own way. Against the background provided by these English country houses, human error and folly play out their perennial comedy.

Finally, these universal characters are presented in a universal context; they are related to universal standards of conduct. There are three of these: virtue, sense and taste. Easily first in importance is virtue, Christian virtue as Jane Austen understood it. She held that it was people's first duty to be unselfish, charitable, honest, disinterested, faithful. But the very seriousness with which she believed this made her think it also imperative to see life realistically. Good notions were to be acted on: you could only be sure that they were good if they passed the test of experience. She shows no enthusiasm for unpractical idealists, feels no sympathy either for soul-stirring emotions that do not in fact serve to make other people better or happier. She was relentlessly anti-sentimental. Nor, though she disapproved of worldliness, did she think it right or sensible to disregard practical considerations. For her, imprudence was never a virtue.

Good sense also led her to believe in making the best of what was inevitably an imperfect existence. This rational belief in the value of contentment went along with her third standard of value, that of taste. Jane Austen thought that how a man lives is only second in importance to what he lives for. Culture and good manners add substantially to human happiness: a wholly satisfactory human being is cultivated and mannerly as well as virtuous and sensible. There are no rough diamonds or noble savages among Jane Austen's heroes and heroines. Life at Mansfield Park had its drawbacks but it was preferable to life at Fanny's Portsmouth home for its superior 'elegance, propriety, regularity and harmony'.

Her belief in these three standards conditions and focuses Jane Austen's picture of humanity. Not one of her characters but is brought before the triple bar of taste, sense and virtue and, if they fail to satisfy their creator on any one of these accounts, smiling but relentless, she passes sentence on them. Marianne Dashwood satisfies on taste and virtue but not on sense; she allowed herself to be a prey to romantic illusions. Mary Crawford is sensible and has excellent taste but she fails to satisfy on virtue. She is worldly, she hesitates to marry the man she loves when she finds he intends to be a country clergyman. Jane Austen applies the standard of taste equally consistently. Vulgar Mrs Jennings turns out to have a warm heart and a good deal of horse-sense and Jane Austen gives her full credit for both; but she continues to get all the fun she can out of Mrs Jennings' vulgarity. Even in apparent distress a character must face the frank judgment of Jane Austen's amused fastidiousness.

> Mrs Musgrove was of a comfortable, substantial size, infinitely more fitted by nature to express good cheer and good humour than tenderness and sentiment: . . . Captain Wentworth should be allowed some credit for the self-command with which he attended to her large fat sighings over the destiny of a son whom alive nobody had cared for. Personal size and mental sorrow have certainly no necessary proportions. A large bulky figure has as good a right to be in deep affliction as the most graceful set of limbs in the world. But, fair or not fair, there are unbecoming conjunctions which reason will patronise in vain – which taste cannot tolerate – which ridicule will seize.

No doubt if Mrs Musgrove's sorrow had been genuine Jane Austen would not have applied the standard of taste so ruthlessly. Even so, there is something startling, if exhilarating, in the cheerful way she notes the comical contrast between Mrs Musgrove's unromantic physique and the pathetic emotion which is supposed to be animating it. Here we see how very much Jane Austen was a child of the eighteenth century. Nothing like these sentences is to be found in the works of any Victorian or post-Victorian English novelist.

For her standards were not of her own making. She applies them so confidently because she takes them for granted, because they were those of the whole society of which she was a member. Jane Austen's morality was the characteristic morality of its brand of Anglicanism; while her belief in the paramount importance of good sense and good taste was the distinguishing mark of its culture. Her standards were representative standards; she spoke for her age. This did not involve any weak concession to convention on her part. Jane Austen always thought for herself and spoke her mind. But her mind agreed with that of her age; she happened to be born with a disposition naturally in sympathy with the point of view of the world in which she found herself. This made life easier for her as a woman; and it was a great piece of luck for her as a writer. Writers who feel themselves at odds with the world they live in tend to be tiresomely aggressive. Just because they feel the wind of opinion against them, they proclaim their unpopular views too loudly and too insistently. Jane Austen wrote with the wind behind her, with an unconscious confidence that she could count on her readers' understanding and sympathy.

In consequence, she feels no need to insist. She was against novels pointing a moral: 'Example, not direct approach,' she said, 'is all a novelist can possibly afford to exhibit.' She practised what she preached. Her stories do exemplify her moral point of view, for this was so much part of her that her every imaginative conception is related to it. But she very seldom moralizes openly. As a matter of fact, she was not tempted to. She saw herself as an entertainer; her primary motive in writing was not to edify but to delight.

She succeeds in doing this and in a unique fashion. Nor was it less so because she spoke as much for her age as for herself. This is because the actual voice in which she speaks is very much her own. The vitality which animates the world of her creation is the vitality of her own highly individual personality. She never copied a character direct from life; partly because she thought to do so was a breach of good manners, but even more because it implied a failure of imagination. 'I am too proud of my gentlemen,' she said, 'to admit that they are only Mr K or Colonel B.' Her great characters are each the product of many diverse pieces of observation, selected, assembled and fused together by the action of her individual imagination. Their peculiar vividness and the insight with which they are brought to life bear the unmistakable stamp of her unique vision.

The character of her genius shows also in the shape of her stories. Untaught and unguided, she achieved a mastery of the novel form unequalled by any other English novelist. More often than any other, she solves the chief formal problem confronting them, which is to satisfy the rival claims of art and life, to produce a work which is both a shapely artistic unity and a convincing representation of diverse, untidy reality. Jane Austen's sense of fact and feeling for order were both unusually and equally strong and she took equal pains to meet the demands of both. Not always successfully: there are a few occasions when a character or incident shows up all too obviously as part of the plot's necessary machinery. But far more often the action seems so probable and spontaneous that what is really an artfully planned construction gives the effect of a free, natural growth.

Most of all her individual genius shows itself in the all-pervading presence of her sense of comedy. She contrives to give us a picture of life which appears true to reality and continuously amusing. To take an example, Mrs Allen in *Northanger Abbey* is an accurate portrait of a mild, talkative, empty-headed woman whose company in real life we would find dull. But, introduced to her by Jane Austen, we find ourselves hanging on her words; by some stroke of delightful magic she has been made entertaining. Jane Austen could perform similar feats on even more unpromising material. Examine the account in *Emma* of how the news of Mrs Churchill's death was received at Highbury.

It was felt as such things must be felt. Everybody had a degree of gravity and sorrow; tenderness towards the departed, solicitude for the surviving friends; and in a reasonable time, curiosity to know where she would be buried. Goldsmith tells us that when lovely woman stoops to folly, she has nothing to do but die; and when she stoops to be disagreeable, it is equally to be recommended as a clearer of ill fame. Mrs Churchill, after being disliked at least twenty-five years, was now spoken of with compassionate allowances. In one point she was fully justified. She had never been admitted before to be seriously ill. The event acquitted her of all the fancifulness and all the selfishness of imaginary complaints.

Here is no comic distortion of sad reality. This, we know, is exactly how the news of such a death would be received by such people. Yet we cannot read it without smiling.

Even when Jane Austen is not out primarily to make us smile, she seldom leaves the realm of comedy. She describes Anne Elliot's love for Wentworth with an exquisite sympathy; but this sympathy does not blind her to whatever ironical implications it may have. Anne is sure that when Lady Russell looks out of the carriage in which they are driving, it must have been to gaze at the passing figure of Wentworth. Jane Austen notes with amusement that in reality it is to see what is in a shop window. However intractable her material may seem to be, she manages to tinge it with a comic tone.

This is partly due to the judgment with which she chooses her angle of vision. She puts herself in a position in which the humorous aspects of her subjects stand out most obviously so that by only setting out the facts in their unemphasized sobriety, she can make them amusing. Mrs Churchill's death had its solemn aspects; but they were not noticeable from the point of view from which Jane Austen looks at it. Comedy is also implicit in the manner in which she tells her story. Her gay astringent irony, her gleeful quickness to perceive the comic aspects of character and situation, embody themselves in her actual choice of words, crisp turn of phrase, in the lively rhythms of her sentences.

Mrs Ferrars was a little thin woman, upright, even to formality, in her figure, and serious even to sourness, in her aspect. Her complexion was sallow and her features small, without beauty, and natural, without expression; but a lucky contraction of the brow had rescued her countenance from the disgrace of insipidity, by giving it the strong character of pride and ill-nature. She was not a woman of many words: for unlike people in general, she proportioned them to the number of her ideas.

This passage illustrates other characteristics of Jane Austen's genius as exhibited in her writing: its blend of hard-hitting and a light touch, its sedulous avoidance of the slipshod, the inflated, the cliché – particularly the kind of cliché popular among the novelists of her day. Writing to advise her niece Anna about a story she had written, Jane Austen comments in humorous horror:

> Devereux Foresster's being ruined by his vanity is extremely good; but I wish you would not let him plunge into a 'vortex of Dissipation'. I do not object to the Thing, but I cannot bear the expression – it is such thorough novel slang – and so old, that I dare say Adam met with it in the first novel he opened.

Her dislike of the slipshod and the inflated was as much moral and personal as it was artistic. Indeed, though she took such pains to keep them apart, the woman and the author were unmistakably one and the same person. To her acquaintances, her books may have come as revelations of an unsuspected literary gift: but they can have disclosed no surprising feelings and opinions, no unexpected strain of thought and imagination. Jane Austen the woman and Jane Austen the artist were of a piece. The delicate orderly precision apparent in her handwriting and her needlework appear also in the design and execution of her novels: she judges real people in her letters by the same standards as she judges imaginary characters in her stories. The very fact that these are so little autobiographical is evidence of the same reserve and vigilant discretion that we notice in her letters. Both novels and letters too are marked by similar limitations. The shyness that made her poem about Mrs Lefroy curiously stilted also hampered her when she came to write a fictional scene demanding a similar expression of heightened feeling. Such scenes are few; and this also is in keeping with what we know of her personal character. The modesty and good sense that led her to accept the limitations imposed on her by life led her also to accept the limitations imposed on her by the nature of her talent.

Finally, the view of human life that marks her books is directly related to her character and to her history. Innate in her was a tough, sharp-sighted intelligence that seems to have stopped her from ever entertaining any illusions about human nature. But she was also born with a good temper and an affectionate heart and had grown up in a happy home as part of a lively, united, appreciative family. Consequently and in spite of the fact that by thirty-four years old she had experienced her share of the troubles inseparable from the human condition, she had acquired a built-in confidence in living. This enabled her to combine, alike in her life and in her art, a robust ironic realism of outlook with an unshaken but rational belief in the existence of human virtue and the possibility of human happiness.

PART III

8

Growing Fame

During 1810, Jane Austen temporarily disappears from view: no letter or record of her survives. But we know that she was fully occupied in revising *Sense and Sensibility* and, *Pride and Prejudice*. By the New Year, *Sense and Sensibility* had been accepted by the publisher and dispatched to the printer. Henry Austen seems to have been the intermediary between her and her publisher. He lived in London and was likely to be more in touch with the literary world. In April 1811, when the proofs had come, Jane Austen went up to stay with him and Eliza. They met at their cousin Cooke's house; and, as she says with affectionate admiration, 'after putting life and wit into the party for a quarter of an hour', he took her to his London house in Sloane Street. Perhaps we should say his house near London; for, in those days, Sloane Street was in a pleasant residential suburb of the capital, separated from it by green fields, through which Jane could speak of 'walking to London' to do some shopping. She enjoyed shopping; she enjoyed her visit altogether. Once again we hear her voice, telling the news to Cassandra in vivacious tones, saying how much she liked going to the shops, to the theatre, to an exhibition of pictures: she found the visitors there more interesting than the paintings: 'My preference for men and women always inclines me to attend more to the company than to the sight,' she said. She also saw some social life. Henry and Eliza gave a musical party while she was with them, where, after an excellent supper, sixty-six people were entertained by professional performers. Jane professed to enjoy the music, but she seems to have spent most of her time in conversation and surrounded by gentlemen, with whom she managed, in spite of her reputation for silence, to have got on well enough to satisfy such modest hopes of social success as she might still cherish. She heard that a Mr Knatchbull had described her as a pleasing-looking young woman. 'That must do,' she remarked contentedly to Cassandra. 'One cannot pretend to anything better now, thankful to have it continue a few years longer!'

Henry's social gifts and the continental connections of Eliza, late Comtesse de Feuillide, made their circle more varied than anything Jane encountered elsewhere. In particular, it meant that she spent time with members of the French colony. She liked these foreigners, so far as her sturdy British prejudices allowed her to. 'The old Comte d'Entraigues,' she says of one of them, 'is a very fine-looking man with quiet manners, good enough for an Englishman and, I believe, a man of great information and taste . . . if he would but speak English, I would take to him!' She also came across several of her many cousins, near and distant, in particular a Miss Payne who amused her by chattering away about a friend of hers called Lady Catherine Brecknell. 'She is most happily married,' Jane related to Cassandra, 'Mr Brecknell is very religious and has black whiskers.' None of these unaccustomed delights however – neither theatre, nor pictures, nor parties – were enough to distract her attention from her concern with the proofs and publication of her book. 'No indeed!' she exclaims, 'I am never too busy to think of *Sense and Sensibility* and can no more forget it than a mother can forget her sucking child.'

May saw her back at Chawton to help entertain a succession of relations: James's daughter Anna, Henry and Eliza and, most important of all, Charles Austen back after seven years away and bringing with him an unknown wife Fanny and two little daughters. All three newcomers made a pleasant impression and Charles, though looking older, was otherwise unchanged and as delightful as ever. Cassandra was away at Godmersham part of the summer:

Rear-Admiral Charles Austen

Jane sent her her customary chronicle, giving news of the family, the neighbours, the garden and the weather. Once however she does refer to public
affairs and characteristically. It is in connection with a battle in the Peninsular
Campaign. 'How horrible it is,' she confides to Cassandra, 'to have so many
people killed and what a blessing one cares for none of them.' There is a
bracing Dr Johnson-like realism about this. Jane Austen did not try to blind
herself to the horrors of war: but neither did she try to pretend that she was not
glad that none of her brothers – for they were the people she cared for –
figured in this particular list of casualties.

II

At last on 30 October came the big event of the year, the publication, by
Thomas Egerton, in three volumes price fifteen shillings, of *Sense and Sensibility*, a novel, By a Lady. The lady in question took special pains to hide the fact
that she was the author. She did not even tell her niece Anna about it: the two
of them, looking at the novels in the Alton Circulating Library, saw *Sense and
Sensibility* lying on the counter. Anna picked up the first volume. 'It must be
nonsense with a title like that,' she said and put it back again. Jane watched her
amused and silent. The public did not share Anna Austen's opinion of the title:
Sense and Sensibility made a definite if not a sensational success. It went into a
second edition and earned its author the then respectable sum of £140.
Though, as might have been expected, it aroused no interest in the new
writers of the Romantic Movement, it was appreciated by the Whig aristocracy, last and glittering representatives of the distinctive culture of the eighteenth century. 'Have you read *Sense and Sensibility*?' writes charming Lady
Bessborough to her lover, Lord Granville Leveson-Gower. 'It is a clever
novel. They were full of it at Althorp, and, though it ends stupidly, I was
much amused by it.' I wonder why Lady Bessborough thought the end
stupid. Perhaps she had herself yielded too readily to the call of passion to
believe that Marianne Dashwood, one of the book's two heroines, could be
happily married to Colonel Brandon, a man she esteemed rather than loved
and who wore a flannel waistcoat.

   In fact, the end of the book is the logical conclusion of its theme, which is
that a life guided by reason and self-control, as exemplified in the story of
Elinor Dashwood, is more likely to lead to happiness than one guided by
feeling and imagination, as exemplified in the story of her sister Marianne. In
spite of being revised, *Sense and Sensibility* still has some of the weaknesses of
an early work: the two heroes, Ferrars and Brandon, lack life and individuality; all too obviously they have been invented to serve the purpose of

the plot. All the same, compared with most novels, the book is a masterpiece, beautifully designed, executed with complete assurance and containing in Marianne a wonderful portrait – the only one Jane Austen ever drew – of a girl in the grip of passion. Further it shows her peculiar power to combine the light and the profound, the particular and the universal. For, while remaining in a comedy key – nothing very dreadful happens in it – it illuminates a fundamental problem of human conduct. The issue that divides Elinor and Marianne is an issue that divides human beings in every age and country.

Jane Austen sides with Elinor: the book states her own scale of values. Otherwise there is little in it to help the biographer. But I do detect a note of personal reminiscence in the passage commenting on Lady Middleton's feelings about the Dashwood sisters.

> Though nothing could be more polite than Lady Middleton's behaviour to Elinor and Marianne, she really did not like them at all. Because they neither flattered herself nor her children, she could not believe them good-natured; and because they were fond of reading, she fancied them satirical: perhaps without exactly knowing what it was to be satirical; but that did not signify. It was censure in common use, and easily given.

Here, surely, is Jane Austen guessing at what the less intelligent of her neighbours are likely to have felt about herself and Cassandra.

The follies consequent on a too 'Romantic' view of life were a main inspiration of Jane Austen's early work. They are the subject of the best of her juvenile burlesques and gave her the first idea for the novel called *Susan* which had been offered in 1803 to Crosby the publisher and which she had asked him to return in 1809. He had made difficulties about this with the result that it was not published till after her death under the new title of *Northanger Abbey*. But it is clearly an expression of an early literary phase of hers that it is more natural to consider it here. It satirizes only a superficial aspect of the Romantic Movement; the heroine, Catherine Morland, sometimes makes a fool of herself because she expects life to be like the tales of romantic terror which are her favourite reading. It is never 'serious' comedy in the way that *Sense and Sensibility* is. Starting as a skit in Jane Austen's teenage manner, it soon turns into a brief light-hearted story of ordinary life. Its very light-heartedness makes it the most lightweight of her novels: but within its limits it is a triumphant success, for it consists entirely of her comedy at its most high-spirited and sparkling. Nor is it ever so light as to lose contact with the solid earth of her ironic sense of reality. Characters, like Mrs Allen and the Thorpe family, are as real as they are comic: while, though the story concludes with the marriage of the hero and heroine, Jane Austen avoids the insipidity of a conventional happy ending by pointing out, with demure amusement, that the hero would not have fallen in love with the heroine had he not happened to notice that she was in love with him. Jane Austen comments: 'It is a new circumstance in romance, I acknowledge, and dreadfully derogatory of an heroine's dignity; but if it be as new in common life, the credit of a wild imagination will at least be all my own.'

For the rest, Jane Austen's personal experience is reflected in the accounts of Bath and its pleasures as they appear to a young girl on her first visits there, that is to say, as they might have appeared to Jane herself during the 1790s; while perhaps, who knows, in the talk of Henry Tilney we may hear the accents of Sydney Smith himself! Certainly Henry's conversation is amusing enough to be Sydney's.

III

In the year 1812 Jane Austen the author finished *Pride and Prejudice*, sent it to the publisher and started a new novel, *Mansfield Park*. In the meantime, the life of Jane Austen the woman was diversified by some family events. Her brother Edward's adopted mother, old Mrs Knight, died: thereafter Edward took the name of Knight. 'I must learn to make better Ks,' said his sister Jane. Also the lease of Chawton Great House came to an end and Edward decided not to let it again. Instead he now spent more time at Chawton himself – he was there for some months in the spring and summer of 1812 – and later lent it for a time to his brother Frank. The result for Jane Austen was that she had the pleasure of seeing much more of her brothers and their children, in particular Fanny Knight. This year also showed some growth in her intimacy with her older niece Anna, the daughter of James Austen. Anna had always been a great friend since she had come to stay with her aunts as a child of three after her mother's death. Now she was twenty, the friendship grew closer. A mental affinity discovered itself between them. They were both much interested in writing and reading fiction. Anna used to ride over with her father from Steventon – the direct route from there to Chawton was a track too rough for a wheeled vehicle – for an afternoon visit: Anna often stayed on for several days. These were delightful days spent largely in talking, not always very seriously, about books.

> It was my amusement [Anna afterwards related] during part of a summer visit to the cottage to procure novels from the circulating library at Alton, and after running them over to narrate and turn into ridicule their stories to Aunt Jane, to

her amusement, as she sat over some needlework which was nearly always for the poor. We both enjoyed the fun, as did Aunt Cassandra in her quiet way though, as one piece of nonsense led to another, she would exclaim at our folly, and beg us not to make her laugh so much.

As well as subscribing to the Alton Circulating Library, Jane Austen belonged to a private local literary society. This enabled her to extend the range of her reading. To her surprise, she found herself much enjoying an essay on the military police of the British Empire: less surprisingly, she was delighted by *Rejected Addresses* by the brothers Smith, a collection of parodies of contemporary authors. As much as by the parodies was Jane Austen amused by some of the conversations she had with people about them. She describes

Chawton Great House.
Drawing by Anna Lefroy

one with Mrs Digweed, an acquaintance since the Steventon days, who had always been an object of mirth to the Austen sisters: Jane Austen's account of this particular talk suggests the reason for this.

> Upon Mrs Digweed's mentioning that she had sent *Rejected Addresses* to Mr Hinton, I began talking to her a little about them, and expressed my hope of their having amused her. Her answer was 'oh dear yes, very much, very droll indeed – the opening of the House, and the striking up of the Fiddles!' What she meant poor woman, who shall say?

In January 1813 *Pride and Prejudice* was published. Its appearance marks the start of the most memorable period of its author's career, that in which her genius, working at its highest power, was, in a succession of books, at last to find complete fulfilment. Not that she ever wrote anything better in its way than *Pride and Prejudice*. As few novels have ever done, it satisfied the rival claims of life and of art. Presenting us with what is, but for an occasional touch of exuberant caricature, a convincing picture of ordinary life, it manages at the same time to be continuously entertaining. Would some people think it so entertaining as to be frivolous, Jane wondered.

> The work is rather too light and bright and sparkling [she remarked ironically to Cassandra]. It wants shade, it wants to be stretched out here and there with a long chapter of sense, if it could be had; if not, of solemn specious nonsense, about something unconnected with the story; an essay on writing, a critique on Walter Scott, or the history of Buonaparte, or anything that would form a contrast.

On the whole, she said, she was vain enough to be satisfied with it. She had reason to be. A sustained exhibition of Jane Austen's comedy at its highest and finest, *Pride and Prejudice* is as amusing as *Northanger Abbey* and as illuminating as *Sense and Sensibility*. For, though it is more strictly a comedy – nothing even potentially tragic occurs in it – it too pierces through the surface accidents of time and place humorously to consider fundamental problems of human character and conduct. Its original title of *First Impressions* indicates its theme, the errors of judgment that arise from trusting to first impressions of people, uncorrected by further experience. Here is another illustration of Jane

Fanny Knight, Jane Austen's niece.
Watercolour by Cassandra Austen

Austen's belief in the paramount importance of paying attention to the guidance of detached good sense, her early-acquired conviction that second thoughts are likely to be better than first.

In one way, *Pride and Prejudice* brings us closer to Jane Austen the individual woman than do any other of her novels. Elizabeth Bennet is the single one of Jane Austen's characters who can, to some extent, be identified with herself. I doubt that she was aware of this, for she says that she thinks Elizabeth 'as delightful a creature that ever appeared in print'; and Jane Austen was too humorous as well as too discreet to speak thus of what she knew secretly to be a self-portrait. Moreover Elizabeth's lack of shyness, her easy confidence and charming audacity, as well as her circumstances, are unlike anything we know of her creator. The fact remains that her humour and the general tone of her talk – and this is true of none of her fellow heroines – are strikingly like Jane Austen's, as they appear in her letters. For, like her, Elizabeth is at the same time a normal girl – interested in social and family life and whether or not she is a success with young men – and also an amused detached observer of the human comedy. More than once she seems to speak with the very voice of her creator; as when she tells Bingley that she does not mind there being fewer characters to study in the country than in town because those in the country 'alter so much that there is something new to be observed in them for ever'; and still more in her comment on Miss Bingley's reverential praise of Mr Darcy.

> 'Mr Darcy is not to be laughed at!' cried Elizabeth. 'That is an uncommon advantage, and uncommon I hope it will continue, for it would be a great loss to me to have many such acquaintance. I dearly love a laugh.'
>
> 'Miss Bingley' said he 'has given me credit for more than can be. The wisest and the best of men, nay, the wisest and best of their actions, may be rendered ridiculous by a person whose first object in life is a joke.'
>
> 'Certainly,' replied Elizabeth 'there are such people, but I hope I am not one of them. I hope I never ridicule what is wise and good. Follies and nonsense, whims and inconsistencies do divert me, I own, and I laugh at them whenever I can.'

These words, taken out of their context, might stand as Jane Austen's motto. Like Elizabeth, she hoped she did not ridicule what is wise and good. But

Anna Lefroy, eldest daughter of The Reverend James Austen.
Painting by R.H.C. Ubstell, 1845

follies and nonsense did divert her; and – again like Elizabeth – she laughed at them whenever she could.

The public laughed with her. *Pride and Prejudice* substantially increased her reputation. It went into a second edition within the year and was enjoyed by a number of distinguished persons, including Sheridan, Warren Hastings and, more surprisingly, Miss Milbanke, the future Lady Byron, who, incidentally, would have been wise to take a lesson from it and not to have trusted to her first impression of Byron! It was also, so her brother Charles said, enthusiastically liked by his fellow naval officers, which says much for the level of culture in the British navy in the early nineteenth century. Charles himself was delighted by *Pride and Prejudice*; so were the rest of the Austen family. Mrs Austen read it aloud to the family circle – rather too fast, thought Jane – amid peals of laughter. Jane Austen responded to her success with unalloyed pleasure. She spoke of *Pride and Prejudice* to Cassandra as her 'darling child', proclaimed her affection for her heroine and demanded that her readers should like her and Darcy, the hero, if they liked no one else in the book. The people in her novels were so real to her that she spoke of them as of living persons. On a visit to London in the following May, she went to two exhibitions of portraits hoping, she said, to find likenesses of the Bennet sisters. She found one of Jane Bennet dressed in green – she had always thought green one of Jane's favourite colours, she said – but none of Elizabeth. 'I can only imagine that Mr Darcy prizes any picture of her too much to like it should be exposed to the public eye. And I can imagine he would have that sort of feeling – that mixture of love, pride and delicacy.'

The occasion of this visit to London was one that might have been expected to have caused a shadow over Jane Austen's spirits. In April Eliza, Henry Austen's wife, had died after a long illness; and Jane had come up to London to keep her brother company in his solitude. As a matter of fact, though the marriage seems to have been reasonably happy, Eliza's death was neither a great shock nor a great tragedy to her bereaved husband. By midsummer Jane, writing to Frank Austen, describes Henry in a slightly apologetic and defensive tone, as in no very distressed state of mind.

Upon the whole [she writes] his spirits are very much recovered. If I may so express myself, his mind is not a mind for affliction. He is too busy, too active, too sanguine. Sincerely as he was attached to poor Eliza moreover, and excellently as he behaved to her, he was always so used to being away from her at times, that her loss is not felt as that of many a beloved wife might be.

Even in May, Henry does not seem to have been so grief-stricken as to damp

Jane's spirits, now raised high by the success of *Pride and Prejudice*. She much enjoyed her stay in London, looking at the portrait exhibitions, driving about the town in a barouche, and she got some mischievous amusement out of a visit to a fashionable girls' school.

> I was shewn upstairs into a drawing room [she related] and the appearance of the room, so totally unschool-like, amused me very much; it was full of all the elegancies – and if it had not been for some naked Cupids over the Mantelpiece, which must be a fine study for the girls, one would never have smelt instruction.

June found her back at Chawton for a happy summer. She finished *Mansfield Park* and sent it off to the publisher. Meanwhile her social life was made delightful by the presence of Edward and his family, established for the first time at Chawton Great House for several months. Jane's affection for her brothers remained the central fact of her personal life. If Henry amused her the most, Edward gave her a peculiar sense of cheerful comfort; and for her naval brothers she continued to cherish a sentiment, tinged with a glow of admiration, kindled by the thought of their heroic profession. To Frank, now a captain and at sea near the Swedish coast, she wrote in July:

> Your profession has its douceurs to recompense for some of its Privations; to an enquiring and observing mind like yours, such douceurs must be considerable. Gustavus and Vasa, and Charles 12th, and Christina, and Linneus – do their Ghosts arise up before you? I have a great respect for former Sweden. So zealous as it was for Protestantism! And I have always fancied it more like England than many Countries.

After this patriotic outburst, she goes on to give him some family news and ends: 'God bless you – I hope you continue beautiful and brush your hair, but not all off. We join in an infinity of Love, Yours very affectionately.'

Frank may not have been so entertaining as Henry, but he was more reliable, as was apparent this very year. Henry was so proud of his sister and her writing that, contrary to what he knew was her wish, he could not help yielding to the temptation to give away her secret. In Scotland that year, for instance, he told some ladies that Jane was the author of *Pride and Prejudice*.

> A thing once set going in that way! [exclaimed Jane to Frank] one knows how it spreads. . . . I know it is all done from affection and partiality – but at the same time let me here again express to you and Mary my sense of the superior kindness which you have shewn on the occasion in doing what I wished.

In spite of her success, Jane's desire that no one should know she was an author remained obsessive. Hence her irritation with Henry. But she loved him too much for it to be anything but momentary.

In September she went back with Edward to Godmersham. It was her first visit for four years and she stayed over two months. She much enjoyed them: as always her main interest was in Edward's children. Fanny of course was her special friend among them and their intimacy had increased at Chawton during the summer. At first, Jane found herself a little critical of the elder boys. Were they not too exclusively absorbed in field sports? Young Edward Knight, back from a holiday in the Lake country, seemed to have noticed none of its natural beauties but only the opportunities offered there for grouse and partridge shooting. Second thoughts however led her to take a kindlier view. She reminded herself that Edward was a good son and a kind brother and unexpectedly religious. When the next Sunday came round, she noticed that he stayed on in church after Matins to take the Sacrament. 'After having much praised or much blamed anybody,' she sighed, 'one is generally sensible of something just the reverse soon afterwards!'

Halfway through the visit, the family party and Jane's pleasure were both increased by the arrival of the Charles Austens. Little Mrs Charles looking neat and 'dear Charles, all affectionate, placid, quiet, cheerful, good humour'. As on former visits too, the party at Godmersham was enlarged by a steady stream of friends and neighbours calling or staying for a night or two; and life there was enlivened in the daytime by walks and expeditions and in the evening by dancing and games and musical parties. Jane enjoyed these decorous gaieties: no less because she was now nearing middle-age and treated as such.

> By the by [she remarked to Cassandra] as I must leave off being young, I find many douceurs in being a sort of chaperone; for I am put on the sofa near the fire and can drink as much wine as I like . . . and Lady Bridges found me handsomer than she expected, so you see I am not so very bad as you might think for.

Handsome or not, she no longer had to worry, as in the past, about social success and dancing partners. Jane Austen, the student of human nature, was now free to concentrate on observing her fellow creatures and thus acquiring material and inspiration for her art.

Throughout the visit, she maintained the good spirits stimulated by the success of *Pride and Prejudice*. Her letters to Cassandra, though in general soberer in tone than those of her youth, are now and again lit up by sparkles of her old agreeable mischief.

Dear Mrs Digweed! I cannot bear that she should not be foolishly happy after a ball.

Only think of Mrs Holder as being dead! Poor woman she has done the only thing in the world she could possibly do to make one cease to abuse her.

Lady Bridges was not what I expected, I could not determine whether she was rather handsome or very plain – I liked her for being in a hurry to have the concert over and get away.

IV

She was back at Chawton by mid-November, after a brief stay in London to see Henry, now moved to a house in Henrietta Street in central London. Thereafter she disappears from our view for several months, during which we know, however, that she had started a new book, *Emma*. In March 1814 her figure emerges again, travelling up from Chawton to London with Henry for another short visit. During her stay, he read *Mansfield Park* presumably in a proof copy. It was different from her earlier books, he said, but not inferior. This was a fair enough comment. In several respects *Mansfield Park* is markedly unlike its predecessors. For one thing the scene is more varied and conceived on a bigger scale: the action extends over eighteen or nineteen years and prosperous, dignified Mansfield Park is contrasted with the Prices' squalid little home in Portsmouth. Secondly, there is a significant difference in the book's tone. This is expressive as always both of the comic and the moral strains inspiring Jane Austen's vision: but the balance between the two strains is different from that of the earlier novels. In *Pride and Prejudice* and *Northanger Abbey* the comic strain predominates: in *Sense and Sensibility* and *Mansfield Park* the moral strain is equally apparent; but in *Mansfield Park* much more formidably so. It remains firmly a comedy; it ends well, it sparkles with humour. But neither the hero nor the heroine are comedy figures: we laugh neither with them nor at them. Moreover the presiding theme of the book is not a comic theme. It can best be described as a comment on the evils of selfishness as presented in the contrast between the unselfish Edmund and Fanny on the one hand, and on the other the crudely selfish young Bertrams and the more subtly selfish young Crawfords. This is not in itself an obvious theme for ironic comedy as were the themes of *Pride and Prejudice* and *Sense and Sensibility*. Jane Austen herself said that *Mansfield Park* had more 'sense' in it than *Pride and Prejudice*, characteristically equating 'sense' with a wise morality. She feared it was therefore less entertaining. She was wrong about this: *Mansfield Park* is extremely entertaining. It is true however that it does suffer at one point from its author's too insistent concern with morality, which

Covent Garden Market: Henry Austen lived nearby in Henrietta Street

leads her, though only on the very last pages, for once to offend seriously against probability. It is unlikely that the cool-headed Henry Crawford with the demands of poetic justice. This required that the sinner should be ever truly loved by eloping with an old flame he had never seriously cared for: it is incredible that selfish, snobbish Mrs Norris would have sacrificed her comforts and social position to spend a dreary old age looking after an outcast niece who had always been bored by her company. Jane Austen commits these offences against probability in order to engineer endings in accordance with the demands of poetic justic. This required that the sinner should be punished for his sin: Mrs Norris must suffer for her misdoings and Henry Crawford must act in such a way as to cut him off irretrievably from Fanny.

Mansfield Park, then, is not so faultless a book as *Pride and Prejudice*. But it makes up for this by its greater variety of scene and mood and the greater depth and subtlety of its psychological insights. Henry and Mary Crawford and their relations with Edmund and Fanny are studies of complex character

and complex feeling such as we find in none of Jane Austen's earlier books. Nor is there anything in them like her vivid accounts of Fanny's solitary unhappiness as a child or of the ugly sordidness of her home at Portsmouth.

The public appreciated the merits of *Mansfield Park*: the first edition was sold out before the end of the year. Most authors write with a reader or a group of readers in mind. Jane Austen's had always been her family and friends. Their opinions of *Mansfield Park*, though in general favourable, were so varied that, detachedly and for her own amusement, she drew up a record of them. These opinions are in character with the persons who held them. It is not surprising to learn that her mother, who so much loved a joke, should prefer *Pride and Prejudice* and find Fanny Price insipid; nor that the more severe but humorous Cassandra should approve of Fanny but delight in the splendid stupidity of Mr Rushworth. To the opinions of her family, Jane Austen added some reported to her as held by acquaintances – especially if they struck her as comic: Miss Pope's, for instance, who liked the book because 'it was so evidently written by a gentlewoman' or that of Miss Augusta Bramstone who had thought both Miss Austen's previous books 'downright nonsense' but, having finished the first volume of *Mansfield Park*, 'flattered herself she had got through the worst'.

In the second half of 1814, Jane Austen went to stay twice more with Henry. Her letters during these three London visits are cheerful enough, with their news about the latest fashions – long sleeves for the evening and black ribbon trimmings for a lilac gown – together with a good deal of gossip; about a young Mr Wyndham who may or may not be in love with Fanny Knight and Mary Oxenden who 'instead of dying, is going to marry William Hammond'; also descriptions of visits to the play, including one to see Miss O'Neill, a fashionable tragedienne with a reputation for moving her audience to tears. It took more than Miss O'Neill to have such an effect on Jane Austen. 'I took two pocket handkerchiefs,' she told Anna, 'but had very little occasion for either. She is an elegant creature, however,' she added, 'and hugs Mr Younge delightfully.'

Eliza O'Neill, 'a fashionable tragedienne' of the period

V

To her biographer, the most interesting documents of this year are her letters to her nieces, Fanny Knight and Anna Austen. Her friendship with them was a chief pleasure of her later life and her letters to them – she was to go on writing them intermittently for the rest of her days – are among her best. They are unlike those she wrote to other people for they are the expression of a different kind of relationship. Her tone in them is the easy intimate tone of one writing to relations who she has known since they were children. Yet it differs from to relations whom she has known since they were children. Yet it differs from news; she takes for granted that Cassandra will want to hear from her and – except for an occasional joke – she does not deliberately set out to make herself agreeable. She was not so sure that her nieces would want to hear from her, so she does set out deliberately to make herself agreeable to them. The consequence is that her letters to them, though never so impishly amusing as she sometimes dares to be to Cassandra, are more charming. Indeed it is from them that we get the best idea of the charm that so many of her relations mention when speaking of her. Particularly is this true of her letters to Fanny Knight. Fanny – 'almost a sister', as she had described her to Cassandra – kept a special place in Jane Austen's heart. This cannot have arisen from a sense of affinity. The youthful Fanny, from the few hints that have come down to us, was very different from her Aunt Jane, a more Victorian type, sentimental, shockable and not noticeably humorous. Perhaps it was the very contrast between Fanny and her unillusioned, ironical self that drew Jane Austen to her. From the time she grew up Fanny seems continuously to have been involved in affairs of the heart, in love at one moment, out of love the next. Because she was motherless, she used to turn, during these emotional crises, to her Aunt Jane, pouring out her perplexities but asking that they should be kept a secret from her Aunt Cassandra, whom, presumably, she judged less sympathetic. Jane agreed to keep the secret: and, at once touched and amused, did her best to respond, answering in long letters in which she discussed the various aspects of Fanny's love dramas. Here are extracts from the letters of this year, written to Fanny who was uncertain whether or not to accept the proposals of Mr John Plumtre, a suitor eligible both morally and intellectually but with whom she is not sure if she is sufficiently in love. Jane is inclined to press the advantages of the match.

> Upon the whole, what is to be done? You certainly have encouraged him to such a point as to make him feel almost secure of you – you have no inclination for any other person – His situation in life, family, friends and above all his character – his uncommonly amiable mind, strict principles, just notions, good habits – all that you know so well how to value. All that really is of the first importance – everything of this nature pleads his cause most strongly. You have no doubt of his having superior Abilities – he has proved it at the University – he is I dare say such a scholar as your agreeable, idle Brothers would ill bear a comparison with. Oh! my dear Fanny, the more I write about him, the warmer

my feelings become, the more strongly I feel the sterling worth of such a young Man and the desirableness of your growing in love with him again. I recommend this most thoroughly. There are such beings in the World perhaps, one in a Thousand, as the Creature You and I should think perfection. Where Grace and Spirit are united to Worth, where the Manners are equal to the Heart and Understanding. But such a person may not come in your way, or if he does, he may not be the eldest son of a Man of Fortune, the brother of your particular friend, and belonging to your own county. Think of this Fanny. Mr J.P. has advantages which do not often meet in one person. His only fault indeed seems Modesty. If he were less modest, he would be more agreeable, speak louder and look Impudenter; and is not it a fine Character of which Modesty is the only defect?

Do not be frightened from the connection by your Brothers having most wit. Wisdom is better than Wit, and in the long run will certainly have the laugh on her side; and don't be frightened by the idea of his acting more strictly up to the precepts of the New Testament than others. And now, my dear Fanny, having written so much on one side of the question, I shall turn round and entreat you not to commit yourself further, and not to think of accepting him unless you really do like him. Anything is to be preferred or endured rather than marrying without Affection; and if his deficiencies of Manner &c &c strike you more than all his good qualities, if you continue to think strongly of them, give him up at once.

The next letters show Jane still more worried lest her words should have encouraged what might turn out to be an unhappy marriage.

Now my dearest Fanny, I will begin a subject which comes in very naturally. You frighten me out of my wits by your reference. Your affection gives me the highest pleasure, but indeed you must not let anything depend on my opinion. Your own feelings and none but your own, should determine such an important point. So far however as answering your question, I have no scruple. I am perfectly convinced that your present feelings supposing you were to marry now, would be sufficient for his happiness; but when I think how very, very far it is from a Now, and take everything that may be, into consideration, I dare not say 'Determine to accept him.' The risk is too great for you, unless your own Sentiments prompt it. You will think me perverse perhaps; in my last letter I was urging everything in his favour, and now I am inclining the other way; but I cannot help it; I am at present more impressed with the possible Evil that may arise to you from engaging yourself to him – in word or mind – than with anything else.

I should not be afraid of your marrying him; with all his worth, you would soon love him enough for the happiness of both; but I should dread the continuance of this sort of tacit engagement, with such an uncertainty as there is, of when it may be completed. Years may pass before he is Independent. You like him well enough to marry, but not well enough to wait. The unpleasantness of appearing fickle is certainly great – but if you think you want Punishment for past Illusion, there it is – and nothing can be compared to the misery of being bound without Love, bound to one, and preferring another!

Certainly these extracts are in a different tone to what we have heard from Jane Austen before: more excited, more demonstrative and touched, though playfully, with a note of tenderness never heard in her letters to Cassandra. No doubt this is because Fanny to her is still partly a child; also any more tender passages occurring in earlier letters are just those which Cassandra might have destroyed as too intimate to be seen by the eyes of a stranger. But it also looks as if with the years Jane had grown less inhibited. She is also less confident than in her youth, particularly in her attitude to love and marriage. Her actual opinion about them has not altered: she still holds the view that love should be a 'rational' passion, inseparable from esteem and respect for the character of the person loved. But observation, and possibly her own experience with the luckless Harris Bigg-Wither, have warned her of the dangers of marrying for purely unsentimental reasons. She has grown aware that marriage without love all too often leads to love without marriage. 'Nothing can be compared to the misery of being bound without Love,' she cries, 'bound to one, and preferring another!' Other statements in these letters reflect Jane Austen's mature conclusions about life, especially her conviction that religious principle is the basis of all right thinking and doing; she was anxious lest Fanny should think – as well she might living in so amusing a family as the Austens – that wit and humour were qualities as important as virtue. This stress on the claims of virtue did not however mean any weakening in the sensible cheerfulness of Jane Austen's general outlook. Fanny, she says, is not to worry about the effect refusing him may have on Mr Plumtre's spirits: 'It is not a creed of mine,' she remarks, 'as you will be well aware, that such sort of disappointments kill anybody.'

Any letters Jane Austen may have written to Fanny during the following eighteen months are lost. The next, written in 1817, show that Fanny's love problems are not over. Mr Plumtre has disappeared from the scene; but she is now exercised as to whether she should marry another eligible gentleman, Mr Wildman of Chilham Castle, while her heart is still half hankering after another admirer unnamed. Jane Austen replies, declaring herself opposed to the unnamed admirer on what seem the reasonable grounds that he has no money, that his brothers and sisters are like horses and finally that she doubts whether Fanny is really in love with him. By this time she has clearly become unable to take Fanny's incessant fluctuations of feeling seriously. But she is as fond of her as ever: fondness and amusement mingle in the tone in which she addresses her.

> My Dearest Fanny,
>
> You are inimitable, irresistible. You are the delight of my life. Such letters, such entertaining letters as you have lately sent! Such a description of your queer little heart! Such a lovely display of what Imagination does. You are worth your weight in Gold or even in the new Silver Coinage. I cannot express to you what I have felt in reading your history of yourself, how full of Pity and Concern and Admiration and Amusement I have been. You are the Paragon of all that is Silly and Sensible, commonplace and eccentric, Sad and Lively, Provoking and interesting. Who can keep pace with the fluctuations of your Fancy, the Capprizios of your Taste, the Contradictions of your Feelings? You are so odd! and all the time so perfectly natural – so peculiar in yourself, and yet so like everybody else! It is very, very gratifying to me to know you so intimately. You can hardly think what a pleasure it is to me, to have such thorough pictures of your Heart. Oh! what a loss it will be when you are married. You are too agreeable in your single state, too agreeable as a Niece. I shall hate you when your delicious play of Mind is all settled down into conjugal and maternal affections.
>
> Mr J.W. frightens me. He will have you: I see you at the Altar. . . . He must be wishing to attach you. It would be too stupid and too shameful in him, to be otherwise; and all the Family are seeking your acquaintance. Do not imagine that I have any real objection. I have rather taken a fancy to him than not, and I like Chilham Castle for you; I only do not like you should marry anybody. And yet I do wish you to marry very much, because I know you will never be happy till you are; but the loss of a Fanny Knight will be never made up to me; My 'Affectionate Niece F. G. Wildman' will be but a poor Substitute.

Jane Austen need not have worried; within a short time Mr Wildman has cooled off and seems even to be transferring his attentions to a Miss Jemima Branfill.

> I have pretty well done with Mr Wildman [Jane comments]. By your description he cannot be in love with you, however he may try at it, and I could not wish the match unless there was a great deal of Love on his side. I do not

know what to do about Jemima Branfill. What does her dancing away with so much spirit, mean? that she does not care for him, or only wishes to appear not to care for him? Who can understand a young Lady!

Another week sees yet another change. Fanny, having decided that she does not love Mr Wildman, feels now comfortable enough with him to lend him one of her aunt's novels, but she does not tell him who is the author: so he had no scruple in saying that he did not think much of it. Jane, hearing this, commented:

I am very much obliged to you my dearest Fanny for sending me Mr Wildman's conversation. I had great amusement in reading it, and I hope I am not affronted and do not think the worse of him for having a Brain so very different from mine; but my strongest sensation of all is astonishment at your being able to press him on the subject so perseveringly – and I agree with your Papa, that it was not fair. When he knows the truth he will be uncomfortable. You are the oddest Creature! Nervous enough in some respects, but in others perfectly without nerves! Quite unrepulsible, hardened and impudent. Do not oblige him to read any more. Have mercy on him, tell him the truth and make him an apology. He and I should not in the least agree of course, in our ideas of Novels and Heroines; pictures of perfection as you know make me sick and wicked – but there is some very good sense in what he says, and I particularly respect him for wishing to think well of all young ladies; it shews an amiable and a delicate Mind. And he deserves better treatment than to be obliged to read any more of my Works.

Jane Austen's letters to Fanny are not confined to the subject of love troubles. She also sought to entertain her with gossip; about Mrs Deedes, exhausted by frequent childbearing, – 'I would recommend to her and Mr Deedes the simple regime of separate rooms' is Jane's practical advice – and on the trouble that Mrs Milles has caused by dying on an inconvenient day:

Poor Mrs Milles that she should die on a wrong day at last, after being about it so long! . . . I hope her friendly, obliging social spirit, which delighted in drawing people together, was not conscious of the diversion and disappointment she was occasioning. I am sorry and surprised that you speak of her as having little to leave and must feel for Miss Milles . . . single women have a dreadful propensity for being poor – which is one very strong argument in favour of matrimony.

It is to be wondered whether Fanny appreciated these more humorous passages in her aunt's letters. Anna Austen certainly would have done: there are more of them in Jane's letters to her. These are different both in tone and subject matter from those to Fanny: less demonstrative and they do not discuss Anna's love life. It was not that she lacked one. Pretty and animated, with the dark eyes and aquiline features of the Leigh family, she attracted young men and, because she was more adventurous than Fanny, got more deeply entangled with them: so much so as sometimes to be the subject of unfavourable comment among her older relations. But, perhaps because she feared her Aunt Jane might not wholly approve of her conduct in these matters, she did not ask her for advice about them. On the other hand she did ask her advice about literary matters. It was their common interest in novels that had led them to becoming such friends during the last few years. Now in 1814 Anna had begun herself to write a novel entitled *Enthusiasm* – later changed to *Which is the Heroine?* Regularly, when she finished each instalment of her story, Anna would send it off to Jane Austen for comment. Jane was as concerned to help Anna in her literary as Fanny in her amorous difficulties. Some days later a long letter from her would arrive back with detailed criticism and advice, the fruit of her own experience as a novelist. Indeed these letters are our chief, almost our only, source of information about Jane Austen's views on the subject of her art. It is from them we learn the paramount importance she laid on making a story credible and probable. It is Anna she advises not to write about people and places of which she has no personal experience. It is Anna she warns against using cliché phrases.

None of this advice is given in an authoritative or patronizing tone. On the contrary: 'If you think differently however do not mind me' so she ends some paragraphs of criticism. Indeed her manner is a model to be copied by any older writer advising a younger. She speaks to Anna as an equal, is truthful but appreciative, practical but not over-serious; as when she writes, after naming a number of contemporary novelists, 'I have made up my mind to like no novels really but Miss Edgeworth's, yours and my own' or, referring to a character in Anna's story:

St Julian's History was quite a surprise to me; You had not very long known it yourself I suspect – but I have no objection to make to the circumstance – it is very well told – and his having been in love with the Aunt, gives Cecilia an additional interest with him. I like the Idea: a very proper compliment to an Aunt! I rather imagine indeed that Nieces are seldom chosen but in compliment to some Aunt or other. I daresay Ben was in love with me once, and would never have thought of you, if he had not supposed me dead of a scarlet fever.

The name of Ben reminds us that Anna's life during this period was not only occupied in novel writing. After a brief abortive engagement early in 1813 to a Mr Terry – it seems she had only accepted him because she was bored at home after her younger brother had gone back to school – she announced in September 1814 that she was going to marry Ben Lefroy, son of the Madam Lefroy who had played so important a part in Jane Austen's early life. Jane had heard the news of the engagement with doubtful feelings.

> I believe he is sensible [she told Cassandra], certainly very religious [he was going to be a clergyman], well-connected and with independence. There is an unfortunate dissimilarity of taste between them in one respect which gives us some apprehension, he hates company and she is very fond of it: this, with some queerness of temper on his side and much unsteadiness on hers is untoward.

Certainly Ben Lefroy's temper was queer enough to lead him to hesitate, during the following year, both about marriage and about becoming a clergyman. However November 1814 saw him united to Anna at Steventon Church. Like that of Emma and Mr Knightley, it was a quiet wedding – Mrs Elton would have described it as 'a most pitiful business'. But like Emma's, it was the prelude to a happy marriage. Three years later Ben Lefroy, having overcome his other hesitations, was ordained. Meanwhile, the newly married couple spent the first year of marriage at Hendon, where Anna went on writing her novel and corresponding with Jane Austen about it. In the autumn of 1815, the Lefroys moved back to settle at a house called Wyards within walking distance of the village of Chawton. This, though no doubt a pleasure for them, has been a loss to posterity; for it meant that Jane wrote Anna no more letters.

In 1815 we get our first glimpse of another correspondence with another niece. This could not be conducted on quite the same terms as those with Fanny and Anna, for this niece was only ten years old. Caroline, daughter of the Reverend James Austen by his second marriage, was more like her half-sister Anna than she was like Fanny Knight. Pretty, humorous and of a literary turn, she had from an early age spent much time at Chawton, delighted by her Aunt Jane, and by the games she invented for children and the stories she told to them. As she grew older, Caroline, like Anna, took to writing stories herself; and she too showed them to Jane Austen who discussed them with her and who, when they were separated, wrote to her about them. 'In addressing children, she was perfect,' recollected Caroline. Indeed, the tone of the letters, though unmistakably Jane Austen's, was delicately modified to suit her child correspondent.

My Dear Caroline,

I wish I could finish stories as fast as you can. I am much obliged to you for the sight of Olivia, and think you have done for her very well: but the good-for-nothing Father, who was the real author of all her faults and sufferings, should not escape unpunished. I hope he hung himself, or took the surname of Bone or underwent some direful penance or other.

Yours affect.
J. Austen.

Caroline spent so much time writing stories that Jane Austen began, a little guiltily, to worry lest she had encouraged her niece to waste energy on them and to think that she would be better occupied in improving her mind by serious reading. In the end she even advised her to give up writing altogether until she was older.

VI

But I am anticipating. These later letters to her nieces have taken us on to a later phase of Jane Austen's history. Returning to the end of 1814, we find her still at Chawton and still occupied in writing *Emma*. She finished it in March 1815. Her creative energy was now in full flood and, within a few months, she had begun on yet another novel, *Persuasion*. In September she went to London to stay with Henry now domiciled in Hans Place – restlessly he had moved house again – and to see about the publication of *Emma*. This was with a new publisher, John Murray, famous as the friend of Byron. She had intended her visit to be a short one. Suddenly Henry was taken ill; within a few days his life was thought to be in danger. As usual in a crisis, the Austen family feeling demonstrated its solidarity. Summoned by Jane, James, Edward and Cassandra were soon at Henry's bedside. After a week he had recovered enough for the brothers to go home again: Cassandra followed them soon after. Jane remained till later in December to look after the most winning and entertaining of her brothers. Henry's illness led to an episode in Jane's life that was gratifying, surprising and, in the event, a little comical. One of the doctors she had consulted – there seem to have been several – was also a doctor to the Prince Regent who, if no model of masculine virtue, was a man of considerable literary sensibility. He had read and enjoyed all Jane Austen's books and

Edward (Austen) Knight (1768–1852) at the time of his Grand Tour.
An anonymous portrait, 1789

kept a set of them in each of his various houses. Informed by the doctor that Miss Austen was in London, he ordered his librarian, the Reverend James Clarke, to wait on her and show her every attention. As a consequence, Jane Austen found herself being taken on a personally conducted tour round the Royal residence of Carlton House. She is likely to have enjoyed it, for the Reverend Mr Clarke was a character to please anyone who loved a laugh: obsequious, pretentious, inept, with a Collins-like reverence for the nobility and without a ray of humour. Together, we may picture them, he solemnly instructing, she listening in amused silence, as they moved through the meretricious splendours of Carlton House, against which their sober figures stand out in incongruous contrast. During their progress, Mr Clarke unexpectedly informed Miss Austen that, if she had a new book coming out, the Prince Regent wanted her to know that she was free to dedicate it to him. This idea was not one which would naturally have occurred to her; and she delayed answering. On the one hand, the future George IV was hardly the man to be approved of by the author of *Mansfield Park*: indeed two years before she had alluded to him in a letter to Cassandra as a character she 'hated'. On the other hand, she could not but be pleased by praise from so august a quarter. Moreover, bred as a loyal Tory subject of the Crown, she wondered whether such a message from the heir to the throne himself did not amount to a Royal Command which it would be impertinent for her to disobey. After consulting her family and without, it seems, much reluctance, she wrote to Mr Clarke saying she would like to dedicate *Emma* to the Prince Regent.

Mr Clarke must have found Jane Austen a sympathetic personality, for he now proceeded to pursue his acquaintance with her. He presented her with a volume of his sermons and wrote her several letters suggesting subjects for her next novel. These were more curious than promising. The first was 'the Habits of Life and Character and Enthusiasm of a clergyman' fond of literature and with no enemies, but whose story might be an occasion to illustrate the evils of the tithe system. Politely, Jane Austen rejected this unusual suggestion.

> I am quite honoured by your thinking me capable of drawing such a clergyman as you gave the sketch of. But I assure you I am not. The comic part of the

*The Grand Staircase at Carlton House
which Jane Austen visited in 1815 when the
Prince Regent, an admirer of her writing,
heard she was in London*

character I might be equal to, but not the good, the enthusiastic, the literary. Such a man's conversation must at times be on subjects of science and philosophy, of which I know nothing; or at least be occasionally abundant in quotations and allusions which a woman who, like me, knows only her own mother tongue, and has read little in that, would be totally without the power of giving.

She says nothing about the tithe question. A few months later Mr Clarke returned to the attack with a fresh idea. He had just been appointed chaplain to the Prince of Cobourg: would not Miss Austen consider writing an historical romance about the Cobourg Royal Family? Miss Austen congratulated him on his appointment but hoped that it was only a step to the higher preferment, less connected with Court life. 'In my opinion,' she commented with hardly perceptible irony, 'the service of a Court can hardly be too well paid, for immense must be the sacrifice of time and feeling required by it.' His suggestion of a subject for her she once more turned down: it was in this letter that she declared that she could no more write a romance than an epic. Her words seem to have carried conviction, for, from this moment, the name of the Reverend Mr Clarke disappears from our history.

Other persons besides him come forward this year with suggestions to Jane Austen. Many were no more sensible than his and she amused herself by drawing up a synopsis for an imaginary novel which could include all of them. It is extremely amusing but, alas, too long for me to note more than its main features. The chief character is Mr Clarke's virtuous and literary clergyman, complete with his objections to the tithe question: its heroine is his daughter, a character 'perfectly good but without the least wit', who converses with her father in long speeches, elegant language and a tone of 'high serious sentiment'. The plot is dramatic; for the heroine is loved by a villainous young man who persecutes her, ruthlessly driving her and her father from one European country to another, in each of which they are:

. . . always making new acquaintances and always obliged to leave them. . . . The scene would always be changing from one set of people to another but all the good people will be unexceptionable in every respect – there will be no foibles or weaknesses but with the Wicked, who will be completely depraved and infamous – hardly a resemblance of humanity left in them.

During her travels the heroine meets with the hero, also faultless and 'only prevented from paying his addresses to her by some excess of refinement'.

Eventually he overcomes this and marries her. But before this happy event occurs, she and her father:

> . . . at last, hunted out of civilised society, denied the poor shelter of the humblest cottage, . . . are compelled to retreat into Kamschatka where the poor Father, quite worn down, finding his end approaching, throws himself on the ground, and after four or five hours of tender advice and parental admonition to his miserable child, expires in a fine burst of literary enthusiasm, intermingled with invectives against Holders of Tithes.

In substance and manner, this synopsis is strikingly like the skits which Jane Austen wrote as a child. At forty she had not changed much from what she had been at twelve, so far as her sense of fun was concerned.

The Carlton House incident has a further interest as illustrating Jane Austen's growing fame. The Prince Regent had discovered her name and so had many other people. During this visit to London and later, she had several chances to make an appearance in London Society in the role of a literary lion. Unhesitatingly she refused: 'If I am a wild beast I cannot help it, it is not my fault,' she told Cassandra: but she was determined not to let herself be treated as such. There is a story that about this time she was invited to a party to meet Madame de Staël, then the most famous authoress in Europe. Jane Austen refused. As a matter of fact, Madame de Staël was not a woman to have appealed to her. Not only was she notorious for her love affairs, but she was also a talker so compulsive and unrelenting that it was rumoured that the great Goethe himself, on hearing that she was about to visit Weimar, precipitately left it. But, even if Madame de Staël had been celebrated for her chastity and as agreeable as Madame Récamier, Jane Austen would have refused to meet her, had she been invited to do so, as the author of *Pride and Prejudice* and *Mansfield Park*.

In December 1815 *Emma* was published. Its appearance may stand as the climax of Jane Austen's literary career. It is futile to discuss whether it is her 'best' book; preference in such matters is a question of individual taste. But it is at least as good as anything she wrote and it is also her most typical work: that in which her distinctive characteristics show themselves at their purest and most extreme, and in which she most firmly confines herself within the limits set by her experience and the nature of her talent. The cast is all drawn from the country gentry and the action remains consistently on the plane of realistic comedy. There are no near farcical figures as there are in *Northanger Abbey* and *Pride and Prejudice*; but the plot never verges on serious drama, as do those of *Mansfield Park* and *Sense and Sensibility*. Yet *Emma* is as 'profound' a comedy as anything Jane Austen ever wrote. Penetratingly it satirizes a basic human weakness: unconscious self-deception. Emma, the heroine, is likable, well-intentioned, and far more intelligent than most of the people round her; but, because she has always had her own way, she has grown up over-confident, so that she tries to influence the lives of others for what she conceives to be their own good. The story demonstrates how this confidence leads her astray; and all the more because her very energy and liveliness of mind distract her from noticing the truth about other people's motives and feelings and even about her own. It is a subject for irony; and the light of Jane Austen's plays, smiling and devastating, over the whole surface of the book. Emma is its chief object; but even the hero, the almost too admirable Mr Knightley, is not exempt from its amused scrutiny. Though quick to note where Emma is deceiving herself, he is unaware that he himself dislikes Frank Churchill, mainly because he suspects Emma is in love with him. The book's consistency of spirit is equalled by its consistency of form. Every episode and character contributes to further the plot: yet the final effect is not that of a calculated composition but rather of a glimpse of real life caught at a moment when its shifting elements have chanced to group themselves into temporary symmetry.

Jane Austen, never confident about her work, was more uncertain than usual about how *Emma* would be received. 'I am haunted with the idea,' she said, 'that to those readers who have preferred *Pride and Prejudice* it will appear inferior in wit and to those who have preferred *Mansfield Park* inferior in good sense': she also said that she thought she had chosen a heroine whom no one but herself would like. Once again she turned first to her immediate circle for their opinions; once again these proved characteristic. It was to be expected that Anna Austen would like Emma herself and that Fanny Knight should not, that Mrs Austen should be amused by the book but still prefer the more rollicking fun provided by *Pride and Prejudice*. One guesses too that Jane Austen was more amused than surprised by the comment of the egregious Mrs Digweed who remarked that, if she had not known the author, she could hardly have got through the book. Mrs Digweed's reaction was exceptional. Most of the opinions recorded by Jane Austen were extremely favourable. Her brother Frank and several others said they liked it best of all her books on account of its 'peculiar air of nature', that is to say its consistent truth to life.

The general public enjoyed it as much as did the Austen family. It was not found inferior to its predecessors and many readers liked the heroine very much. Indeed the self-effacing Miss Austen was now generally accepted as among the first of living authors. This is shown by the fact that the number of the influential *Quarterly Review* published in March 1816 contained a whole article devoted to her work, unsigned but known to have been written by

Walter Scott, most famous and admired of contemporary novelists. Though he praises *Emma* with some reservations – unaccountably, he suggests that there is perhaps too much of Miss Bates and Mr Woodhouse in it – the general effect of the article is gratifyingly respectful and warmly appreciative. Scott's admiration for Jane Austen was to grow even greater with time. Ten years later he writes in his diary:

> That young lady has a talent for describing the involvements and feelings and characters of ordinary life, which is to me the most wonderful I ever met with. The big Bow-Wow strain I can do myself like any now going; but the exquisite touch which renders ordinary common-place things and characters interesting from the truth of the description and the sentiment is denied to me.

Scott was a discriminating judge of literature. His words, true then, are true still. At his best, he can 'do the big Bow-Wow strain' as well as any novelist who ever lived: while Jane Austen's 'exquisite touch' was and remains unique.

*Walter Scott. Oil painting
by A. Geddes c. 1823*

9

The End

Up to the end of 1815, Jane Austen's Chawton years had been years of growing success and of the happiness that goes with it. Now her luck was to turn and her sky gradually to be overcast with gathering clouds. Clouds of family trouble first of all; Edward Knight had, for the last two years, been involved in a worrying law suit: one of his Knight relations was claiming possession of his Chawton property which provided him, Edward, with two thirds of his income. In the end he was to win his case but in 1815 it had begun to look disturbingly as if he might lose it. At the same time a greater calamity was befalling Henry Austen. The bank, in which he was a partner, failed and in March 1816 he was made a bankrupt. Though he was not to blame for the bank's failure, it was all the same very embarrassing to him; for his relations had, out of family feeling, invested largely in the bank, with the result that both his brother Edward and his Uncle Leigh Perrot now lost considerable sums of money. However Henry's congenital inability to be depressed for long enabled him to get over his misfortune fairly quickly. He decided that banking was not his métier and that, after all, he would do better as a clergyman. Never one to let the grass grow under his feet, he had by the end of the year managed to get himself ordained and to have obtained a curacy at Bentley not far from Chawton where he was soon making a reputation for himself as an eloquent preacher. Jane entered into this new phase of her brother's career with sympathy and relief. But its earlier ups and downs, together with Edward Knight's worries, meant that the family atmosphere during this year was pervaded by disagreeable and unaccustomed feelings of tension and insecurity, which, for the only recorded occasion in the family history, nearly led the Austens to quarrel with each other.

Jane felt the effect of this all the more because she was not in a state of health to resist its impact. For, in the background of her consciousness, there had begun to hover a shadow of a grave, personal anxiety. Early in the year she had begun to suffer occasionally from pains in the back and other mysterious symptoms including inexplicable fits of fatigue and weakness. These symptoms recurred, though never very acutely, on and off during the summer. The doctors could not explain them, but we know now that they showed Jane Austen to be in the early stages of the malady called Addison's disease, at that time fatal.

From the first she seems at moments to have had a mysterious sense that there was something seriously wrong with her; for in the spring she went on a visit to see some old friends, the Reverend and Mrs Fowle, relations of Cassandra's deceased fiancé, at Kintbury in Berkshire. Jane had stayed there in the past; now her hosts noticed, not only that she looked changed and ill, but that she liked to wander about her old haunts and talk about old memories of the place in a 'peculiar manner – as if she did not expect to see them again'. This cannot have been a frequent feeling, let alone a settled conviction, for other accounts of her during the next month describe her as much her usual self: and in her letters she speaks of her illness, if at all, lightly and hopefully. We get the impression that neither health nor family anxieties prevented her from passing what was in many ways an agreeable summer.

Two things added to this agreeability. Her sailor brothers were both back in England and often at Chawton with their families. Affectionate and conversational as ever, they enlivened life at the cottage with their accounts of picturesque foreign scenes and exciting naval exploits and the invigorating glimpses these disclosed of a wider, adventurous, masculine world. Jane Austen's days were also brightened by the frequent presence of yet another member of the younger generation. This time it was not a niece but a nephew, James Austen's son Edward, eighteen years old and about to leave Winchester. He was not exactly a new friend for Jane Austen: she had known him all his life and more intimately since he was fifteen. It was her novels that had brought them closer together. Edward had much enjoyed the first two; but, presumably because he was thought too young, had not been told the secret of their authorship. Some time in 1814, he sent her a poem revealing that he had discovered it.

> No words can express, my dear Aunt, my surprise
> Or make you conceive how I opened my eyes,
> Like a pig Butcher Pile has just struck with his knife,
> When I heard for the very first time in my life
> That I had the honour to have a relation
> Whose works were dispersed through the whole of the nation.
> I assure you, however, I'm terribly glad;

Oh dear, just to think (and the thought drives me mad)
That dear Mrs Jennings' good-natured strain
Was really the produce of your witty brain,
That you made the Middletons, Dashwoods and all,
And that you (not young Ferrars) found out that a ball
May be given in cottages never so small.
And though Mr Collins so grateful for all
Will Lady de Bourgh his dear patroness call,
'Tis to your ingenuity really he owed
His living, his wife, and his humble abode.
Now if you will take your poor nephew's advice,
Your works to Sir William pray send in a trice;
If he'll undertake to some grandees to show it,
By whose means at last the Prince Regent might know it,
For I'm sure if he did, in reward for your tale,
He'd make you a countess at least without fail,
And indeed, if the princess should lose her dear life,
You might have a good chance of becoming his wife.

These lines, with their joyous impudent references to the Prince Regent – what would the Reverend Mr Clarke have thought of them! – recall his Aunt Jane at his age. From this time on Edward Austen was often at Chawton. By 1816 he was as much a special friend of his Aunt Jane as were Anna and Fanny. Indeed he was an attractive personality and of a type she knew best and liked most. Good-looking with a light figure and fair skin, Edward Austen was very much a chip of the old Austen block, cultivated and sociable with a sweet temper, easy responsive manners and a civilized sense of fun. Mentally and socially, he had grown up early and by eighteen he was fully able to appreciate his Aunt Jane and to converse with her on equal terms. She loved his visits – 'as agreeable as ever,' she writes, 'sitting in such a quiet comfortable way making his delightful little sketches' – and responded to his appreciation. Only two of her letters to him are left, both written in 1816: but they show her at her most delightful and vividly convey the particular flavour of their relationship; because he was a male, both a little more formal than that with her nieces and a touch more flirtatious. Here is a passage from the first, written in July:

I am glad you recollected to mention your being come home. My heart began
to sink within me when I had got so far through your letter without its being

Edward Austen-Leigh, Jane Austen's nephew

Powell 1864

mentioned. I was dreadfully afraid that you might be detained in Winchester by severe illness, confined to your bed and quite unable to hold a pen and only dating from Steventon, in order, with a mistaken sort of tenderness, to deceive me. But now, I have no doubt of your being at home, I am sure you would not say it so seriously unless it actually was so. We saw a countless number of postchaises full of [Winchester] Boys pass by yesterday morning – full of future heroes, legislators, fools and villains. You have never thanked me for my last letter which went by the Cheese. I cannot bear not to be thanked. You will not pay us a visit yet of course, we must not think of it. Your Mother must get well first, and you must go to Oxford and not be elected; after that, a little change of scene may be good for you, and your physicians I hope will order you to the sea, or to a house by the side of a very considerable pond.

The significance of the last sentence lay in the fact that Chawton village pond lay just outside Chawton Cottage.

The second letter was written four months later. In the intervening period Edward has left school and, like his sister Anna before him, has been inspired by his aunt's example to begin writing a novel. Jane Austen refers to both these events in her reply: it is in connection with Edward's novel that she gives him the memorable description of her own art which I quoted earlier in this book.

My Dear Edward

One reason I am writing to you now, is that I may have the pleasure of directing to you Esquire. I give you joy of having left Winchester. Now you may own, how miserable you were there; now, it will gradually all come out – your crimes and your miseries – how often you went up by the Mail to London and threw away Fifty Guineas at a Tavern, and how often you were on the point of hanging yourself – restrained only, as some illnatured aspersion upon poor old Winton had it, by the want of a tree within some miles of the city . . .

I wonder when you will come and see us. I know what I rather speculate upon, but I shall say nothing. We think uncle Henry in excellent looks. Look at him this moment and think so too, if you have not done it before; and we have the great comfort of seeing decided improvement in uncle Charles, both as to health, spirits and appearance. And they are each of them so agreeable in their different ways and harmonize so well, that their visit is thorough enjoyment. Uncle Henry writes very superior sermons. You and I must try to get hold of one or two, and put them into our novels; it would be a fine help to a volume; and we could make our heroine read it aloud of a Sunday evening, just as well as Isabella Wardour in *The Antiquary*, is made to read the history of the Hartz

Demon in the ruins of St. Ruth – though I believe on recollection, Lovell is the reader. By the bye, my dear Edward, I am quite concerned for the loss your Mother mentions in her letter; two chapters and a half to be missing is monstrous! It is well that I have not been at Steventon lately, and therefore cannot be suspected of purloining them; two strong twigs and a half towards a nest of my own, would have been something. I do not think however that any theft of that sort would be really very useful to me. What should I do with your strong, manly, spirited sketches, full of variety and glow? How could I possibly join them on to the little bit (two inches wide) of ivory on which I work with so fine a brush as to produce little effect after much labour.

II

During the previous months – and this is another proof that she cannot have been feeling very ill – her 'fine brush' had been active and to great effect. Before he left London to embark on his clerical career, Henry Austen had at last managed to extract from Crosby the publisher the manuscript of the novel later to appear as *Northanger Abbey*, and Jane had been at work bringing it up to date. More important, she had in August finished *Persuasion*. This, so far from showing any weakening of its author's power, is an exquisite master-piece and one in which she breaks fresh ground. Not in any obvious way; Jane Austen realized too well the limitations within which her genius operated to consider venturing beyond them. The world of *Persuasion* is still the world of the country gentry and the book is still a comedy. But its prevailing mood and the atmosphere that pervades it subtly differ from those of her earlier books. Its theme is love; how far should love be restrained by considerations of prudence. Before the book begins, the youthful Anne Elliot, under the influence of Lady Russell, an older and, as she thought, wiser friend, has from motives of prudence broken off her engagement to a young naval officer, Frederick Wentworth. The plot, which ultimately brings the two together again after a period of years, describes how Anne comes to think that she had been mistaken in breaking off the engagement. It is a different kind of subject from any Jane Austen has attempted before; and the spirit in which she treats it suggests a shift in her attitude. A shift, not a reversal; there is no question of Jane Austen turning against her past opinions to adopt the view that prudence is not a virtue and that love should override all other considerations. No – Anne's error had lain in a wrong estimate of Wentworth. She should have realized that his moral and mental qualities were such that it would not have been imprudent, in any good sense of the word, for her to have married him. This moral, though not inconsistent with Jane Austen's fundamental sense of values, presents a new aspect of it and one which shows she has realized more fully than in the past that right feeling is an integral part of good sense. Further, she has, by forty years old, learned that the problems of the heart are too delicate and too momentous to be decided with the unhesitating confidence of her youth. She says of Anne Elliot that 'she had been forced into prudence in her youth, she learned romance as she grew older – the natural sequence of an unnatural beginning.' The tone of this sentence is something new in Jane Austen's work and something self-revealing. It cannot be taken as autobiographical in a direct and factual sense: we have no reason to suppose that Jane Austen herself was ever forced into prudence in her youth. All the same these words of hers do throw light on her thoughts and feelings at this later stage of her life and indicate they were not quite the same as they once had been. As is often the case with clever people, Jane Austen's head had matured sooner than her heart. The young Jane Austen had understood what it was like to be in love – she could not otherwise have described the love story of Marianne Dashwood so convincingly – but she thought it important not to be sentimental about the subject. Unless love was under the firm control of good sense and good principles, she regarded it with a detached even an ironical eye. By middle life her attitude had changed: though she could still regard love with a touch of irony, this was softened by a new mood of pensive sympathy. There is nothing in her previous novels like Anne's answer to Captain Harville who has been maintaining that men are more constant in life than women are.

> 'Oh!' cried Anne eagerly, 'I hope I do justice to all that is felt by you, and by those who resemble you. God forbid that I should undervalue the warm and faithful feelings of any of my fellow-creatures. I should deserve utter contempt if I dared to suppose that true attachment and constancy were known only by woman. No, I believe you capable of every thing great and good in your married lives. I believe you equal to every important exertion, and to every domestic forbearance, so long as – if I may be allowed the expression, so long as you have an object. I mean, while the woman you love lives, and lives for you. All the privilege I claim for my own sex (it is not a very enviable one, you need not covet it) it is that of loving longest, when existence or when hope is gone.'

Anne's words ring in our ears with the poignancy of a personal utterance. Here, for once, it is difficult not to suspect Jane Austen is speaking from experience. Could she have written thus, one wonders, had she never met the unnamed gentleman at Sidmouth and loved him and lost him and – for a time at least – gone on loving him 'when existence or when hope was gone'?

Anne's speech, incidentally, shows a new development in Jane Austen's art as well as in her subject matter. Never before has she expressed strong feeling so effectively. Her mode of doing so is still characteristically cautious. We do not hear Anne openly confessing her love for Wentworth but conveying it, as it were, involuntarily and by implication, in a conversation with Harville whom she does not know very well. None the less, she manages to do so with moving eloquence. Elsewhere, too, in *Persuasion* Jane Austen allows herself to express feeling directly; not only love but the ardent affectionate admiration she felt for the British navy – seeing so much of Frank and Charles this year may have intensified this – and also her love of natural beauty, apparent in her enthusiastic comments on the scenery around Lyme Regis and in her references to the charm of the Upper Cross countryside in autumn, 'that season,' so she speaks of it, 'of peculiar and inexhaustible influence on the mind of taste and tenderness'. Her actual passages of description are slight, no more than brief mentions of 'tawny leaves' and 'withered hedgerows'. Yet they contribute significantly to the book's effect. For – and this too for the first time – Jane Austen relates them symbolically to the human drama: the tender autumnal weather is an image of the tender autumnal sentiment that possesses the heart of the heroine. So also do other elements in the design of *Persuasion* relate to its central subject. Its various episodes – the rash happy marriage of the Crofts, the love enduring through hardship of the Harvilles, the inconstancy of Benwick – all these by contrast or similarity demonstrate the issue of love versus prudence which is the theme of the book, integrating them into what is not just a dramatic but also a spiritual unity. This also is new in Jane Austen's work making *Persuasion* in some ways her most original achievement.

It is not her most perfect. Certain of its characters, notably Lady Russell and Mrs Smith, though playing a crucial part in the plot, lack life and individuality, they are outlines of figures not yet filled in or coloured. Surprisingly, Jane Austen spoke of *Persuasion* as 'ready for publication' but added, without giving any reason, that all the same it was not to be published for another twelve months. To me this suggests that she realized that it was still in need of revision; but, for the time being at any rate, no longer felt up to doing any more to it. For, towards the end of 1816, her illness began to get worse. At first the process was still gradual and intermittent. There were days, even weeks, when the progress of the disease seemed to be arrested; sometimes she even talked of recovery. No doubt this was partly because she believed in looking as much as she could on the bright side of things and also because she thought it tedious and inconsiderate to worry other people, especially her mother and sister, with gloomy complaints. But, even when she had a relapse and had to admit it, she still remained observant, humorous, ready to take an interest in other people's lives, especially in those of her nephews and nieces. Her most charming and animated letters to Fanny Knight were written as late as March 1817: one shows her still feeling lively enough to tease Fanny about her taste for the ideal in fiction. 'You may perhaps like the heroine,' she says to her about Anne Elliot, 'as she is almost too good for me!'

Further – and this is the most important evidence of her continued vitality – her creative impulse was still functioning. Jane Austen the woman might be growing weaker; but the other more essential Jane Austen, the novelist, still felt the urge to express herself in her art. In January 1817, with *Persuasion* out of the way, at least for the time being, she began a new novel, the unfinished fragment to be issued many years later under the title of *Sanditon*. Coming when it did, it is a surprising work. Jane Austen might have been expected to have continued in the new trend she had inaugurated in *Persuasion*, with its note of more pensive and complex sentiment. To do so would surely have been more in harmony with her own mood at this sadder phase of her life. Contrary to expectation however *Sanditon* reads like a reversion to Jane Austen's youth: were it not for a few topical references to Wordsworth and the Battle of Waterloo, we might almost take it for an early work. It consists of a series of vigorous satirical portraits, unrelieved by any touch of sentiment and directed against the same kind of object as she had mocked in her youth, affectation, melodrama, sentimentality, silliness. The spirit of the book is eminently one of tough good sense and it makes unsparing fun – this is noteworthy in view of the author's physical state – of persons who make too much fuss about their health. Altogether, in *Sanditon* we feel ourselves back in the eighteenth century, stylish, sparkling, robust, outspoken.

> Sir Edward's great object in life was to be seductive. With such personal advantages as he knew himself to possess, and such talents as he did also give himself credit for, he regarded it as his duty. He felt that he was formed to be a dangerous man – quite in the line of the Lovelaces. The very name of Sir Edward he thought, carried some degree of fascination with it . . . It was Clara whom he meant to seduce. Her seduction was quite determined on . . . If she could not be won by affection, he must carry her off. He knew his business. Already he had many musings on the subject. If he were constrained so to act, he must naturally wish to strike out something new, to exceed those who had gone before him – and he felt a strong curiosity to ascertain whether the Neighbourhood of Timbuctoo might not afford some solitary house adapted for Clara's reception. But the expense, alas! of measures in that masterly style was ill-suited to his purse; and prudence obliged him to prefer the quietest sort of ruin and disgrace for the object of his affections, to the more renowned.

This is very like a passage from Jane Austen's early writings: it is very unlike one from *Persuasion*. The difference, surely, is the consequence of her declining health. She still wanted to write, but she felt unequal to the task of experimenting whether in matter or manner. Perhaps too she was concerned to avoid any topic involving sad or serious feelings: she needed to keep her spirits up by writing about things that made her laugh. Finally, in her weakness, she returned instinctively to her basic and original source of inspiration. *Sanditon* demonstrates once again that Jane Austen's was primarily a comic genius. In her end was her beginning. As a woman of forty-one in the grip of a mortal disease, she turned for a last inspiration to that irrepressible sense of fun which had stirred her to write as a child of twelve.

Very effectively too; the invalid Jane Austen managed to make *Sanditon*, if less subtle and polished than her finished work, yet still infectiously entertaining. Alas, she could not keep it up. The manuscript suddenly breaks off; its author was too ill to go on with it. Some time in March 1817 Jane Austen the novelist put down her pen. It was to be for ever: since the new year her condition had begun quickly to deteriorate. After January, she felt too weak to go for a walk; for a time she tried taking the air in a donkey carriage; soon however, too exhausted even for this mild form of exercise, she gave up going out at all. Instead she spent her days in bed or in the sitting room, stretched out on an improvised sofa made up of two or three chairs placed together. There was a real sofa in the room – why did not Aunt Jane lie on that the child Caroline asked her. Aunt Jane replied that she found the improvised sofa more comfortable. She did not give her true reason, which was she thought the real sofa should be reserved for her seventy-year-old mother who, if ever she found Jane on it, would certainly insist on giving it permanently up to her.

In other ways, and in order to spare her relations anxiety, Jane tried to make light of her illness. But in fact the growing strain of it had begun to affect her nervous system. This appeared in a brief uncharacteristic loss of self-command. At the end of March, her Uncle Leigh Perrot died. It had always been thought that he would leave his money to his sister, Mrs Austen, and her children, of whom he had always been fond. When the will was read, it turned out that he had left everything, with the exception of some legacies to James Austen and his family, to his wife, the formidable Mrs Leigh Perrot. The rest of the Austens bore the disappointment well enough – 'I expect he thought that I, as older than him, would be likely to die first,' said Mrs Austen philosophically; and Cassandra went off to attend the funeral and see if she could be of any help to her widowed aunt. All that we know of Jane Austen would lead us to expect that she would have behaved with an equal appearance of composure. But she was now in no state to stand any kind of shock. The news of her uncle's will had a violently disturbing effect on her nerves. Left at Chawton, she felt so ill and wretched that she wrote off to Cassandra beseeching her to come back at once. She came and Jane immediately felt better; but she was now stricken with a sense of guilt for having acted in a fashion she thought unreasonable and inconsiderate. 'I am the only one of the legatees who has been so silly,' she writes apologetically to her brother Charles, 'but a weak body must excuse weak nerves.'

III

There is no record of her ever breaking down again in this way. But, from now on, the attacks came more and more often and left her each time weaker. Anna and Caroline Austen, over from Wyards, found her in her bedroom sitting by a fire in her dressing gown. Very pale and her voice scarcely rising above a whisper, she nevertheless made an effort to rise and greet them. But after a quarter of an hour she found herself too exhausted to continue the interview. There were days when she felt stronger than this and she then still liked to put on a show of hope and to talk of getting well. But no longer, it seemed, did she believe it. A year before, wandering round the Kintbury garden, she had been visited by a chill premonition of death. Now – after what silent inner conflicts of the spirit we can only guess – she had the calm of one who has faced and accepted the fact that death was coming. Her relations too had ceased to hope for her recovery. Once more and for the last time in this history, the Austen family's solidarity demonstrated its power, as its members joined to support Jane in this supreme crisis of her existence. Luckily, most of them were available. Three of her brothers – James, Henry and Frank – were within riding or walking distance; and hardly a day passed without one of them or of their families going over to Chawton to inquire and offer practical assistance or – if Jane was well enough to see them – to talk to her and amuse her. As for Cassandra, her days and nights were now wholly dedicated to nursing her sister. Her devotion and that of her brothers could not save Jane's life but they were not in vain. A sense of the tender affection surrounding her at the time of her most need comforted and heartened her. She responded demonstratively; the warmth of her feelings had melted the last trace of her Austen reserve. 'As to what I owe her [Cassandra] and the anxious affection of all my beloved family,' she wrote, 'I can only cry over it and pray God to bless them more and more.'

  In the same letter she speaks of resigning herself to trouble, as to something appointed by God. As well as by her family's affection, Jane Austen's spirit was supported by her religious faith. Unobtrusively active throughout her mature life, now, in the last phase of her story, it disclosed its full strength. She mentions religion more often in her later letters than in her earlier, so that some people have thought that her views of it had altered: in particular, they have wondered whether she had come under the influence of the Evangelical Movement, at that time the most vital force in Protestant England. Started more than half a century before by Wesley and Whitefield, it had since swept through the country, establishing in every part of it centres of enthusiastic piety. It had never been the type of religion to appeal to Jane Austen. 'I do not like Evangelicals,' she wrote to Cassandra in 1809. Instinctively she disliked what she called 'noisy religion'; and there was no doubt that Evangelical piety with its emotional preachers and fervent hymn-singing was 'noisy'. It is true to say that seven years later, in one of her letters to Fanny Knight, she does seem to go back on this a little. Fanny had complained that one of her suitors, the eligible Mr Plumtre, had grown so alarmingly pious that she feared he might become an Evangelical. Jane came to his defence:

> As to there being any objection from his goodness, from the danger of his becoming Evangelical, I cannot admit that [she said]. I am by no means convinced that we ought not all to be Evangelicals and am at least persuaded that those who are so, from reason and feeling, must be happiest and safest.

These remarks are less significant than may appear. Jane Austen never adopted either the beliefs or the practices that distinguished the Evangelicals from other Christians: she never uses their characteristic phrases or speaks in praise of their leaders. On the contrary, in a later letter she refers to the sermons of an Evangelical cleric called Cowper with dislike, because they were all about Regeneration and Conversion, two typical Evangelical terms and both implying a belief that religion was as much a matter of feeling as of right conduct, a view with which Jane Austen was thoroughly out of sympathy. When she said to Fanny that perhaps we all ought to be Evangelicals, she meant that too many so-called Christians, including herself, did not live up to the principles of their creed and that, in so far as the Evangelicals did, we ought to imitate them. Jane Austen was noted all her life for not changing her opinions; and this was true of her religious opinions. Always she remained a steady supporter of Anglican Christianity, as taught her by her father, finding all the guidance she needed in the regular and traditional services she attended every Sunday at Chawton Parish Church.

The faith she learned there inspired her during her later years to write some prayers of her own, presumably as part of her private devotions. As examples of the art of prayer-writing, they are nothing remarkable: Jane Austen had no

Chawton Church. Drawing by Anna Lefroy

more talent for writing prayers than she had for writing serious poetry. But the fact that she tried to shows how active and personal her faith was. The prayers themselves shed a light on the nature of her religion. This belonged to the stern rather than to the sweet brand of Christianity; emphasizing how little she thought she lived up to her professed principles and how dependent she feared she would have to be on God's mercy if she was ever to attain salvation. This was not out of character. Herself a realist, Jane Austen recognized – as many professed Christians do not – that Christianity is a realistic religion, with no illusions about the fallen nature of man. Jane Austen was a severe judge of her own moral character and many of her prayers were occupied with contrition and confession. The sins she picked out for especial mention are significant.

> Incline us Oh God! to think humbly of ourselves, to be saved only in the examination of our own conduct, to consider our fellow-creatures with kindness, and to judge of all they say and do with that charity which we would desire from them ourselves.

The author of this is only too well aware that she is likely to be tempted to be uncharitable, the besetting sin of the satirist. However, in general the prayers keep a balance. They are far from being all about sin and repentance. There is also much thanksgiving in them. She reminds herself to be grateful for happiness; and she speaks as one who has had much happiness to be grateful for. Finally and characteristically, she often brings her family into her prayers.

> More particularly do we pray for the safety and welfare of our own family and friends wheresoever dispersed, beseeching thee to avert from them all material and lasting evil of body or mind: and may we by the assistance of thy Holy Spirit so conduct ourselves on earth as to secure an eternity of happiness with each other in Thy Heavenly Kingdom.

She cannot imagine any heaven worth going to in which the Austen family are not reunited to enjoy eternal bliss in each other's company.

IV

In the middle of May new symptoms appeared which the local doctor said he did not understand. Accordingly she was advised to go to Winchester to consult a practitioner with a great reputation called Lyford. James Austen sent over his carriage and one rainy morning, on 24 May, accompanied by Cassandra, Jane set out on her fourteen-mile journey, with Henry and Edward Knight's son William riding on each side of the carriage. Dr Lyford, though secretly he thought there was not much hope, prescribed some alleviating treatment, which meant staying on at Winchester. Lodgings had been found for Jane and Cassandra at College Street, a retired little cul-de-sac close to the grey medieval buildings of Winchester School and within hearing of the drowsy chimes of the great cathedral and the clamorous daws circling its towers, which, two years later, were to echo so hauntingly in the ears of the youthful Keats. Three days after her arrival, Jane wrote to her nephew Edward Austen. This, the last complete letter of hers that we have, gives us an idea of the front which Jane Austen, during her last weeks on earth, chose to present to the world and also, involuntarily, of the very different feelings that lay behind it. The chosen front was deliberately cheerful: yet again she makes light of her illness, jokes about its symptoms, even professes to expect to recover from it. She also says how pleased she is with her lodgings and how grateful to Edward's parents for making her journey so easy.

> I know no way [she writes] my Dearest Edward of thanking you for your most affectionate concern for me during my illness than by telling you myself as soon

as possible that I continue to get better. I will not boast of my handwriting, neither that nor my face have yet recovered their proper beauty, but in other respects I am gaining strength very fast. I am now out of bed from nine in the morning to ten at night – upon the sofa 'tis true – but I eat my meals with Aunt Cassandra in a rational way, and can employ myself, and walk from one room to another. Mr Lyford says he will cure me, and, if he fails, I shall draw up a Memorial and lay it before the Dean and Chapter, and have no doubt of redress from that Pious, Learned and Disinterested Body. Our lodgings are very comfortable. We have a neat little Drawing room with a Bow-window overlooking Dr Gabell's garden. Thanks to the kindness of your Father and Mother in sending me their carriage, my journey hither on Saturday was performed with very little fatigue, and, had it been a fine day, I think I should have felt none; but it distressed me to see Uncle Henry and William Knight, who kindly attended us on horseback, riding in rain almost all the way.

Then, in a final paragraph, her tone changes; to betray – though in quiet controlled words and, as it were, unintentionally – the emotion called up in her by her sense of her true situation; an emotion mingling tender regretful love for those she may be leaving with anxious awe at the thought of the Divine Justice before whom she may, all too soon, have to present herself.

God bless you, my dear Edward. If ever you are ill, may you be as tenderly nursed as I have been, may the same blessed alleviations of anxious sympathising friends be yours, and may you possess – as I dare say you will – the greatest blessing of all, in the consciousness of not being unworthy of their Love. I could not feel this.

This last sentence – revealing as it does her profound feeling of her unworthiness – is poignant; and all the more so for the understated terseness with which it is expressed.

The mood of this letter pervaded her spirit during the six weeks of life that remained to her. Though she suffered little pain, she gradually grew weaker: yet the people around her were struck by how much she managed to appear her customary self: easy, clear-headed, and, on the days she felt better, even playful, able to be amused and, so they said, 'to amuse others even in their sadness'. Her brother Henry noted that she was more than resigned, she was cheerful. Alone, she turned again to writing as a distraction, not stories but letters and, now and again, light verses in the Austen tradition. Meanwhile, she fortified her spirit with frequent prayers and regular religious reading. One or other of her two clergymen brothers, James and Henry, used to read the service with her as an aid to devotion

College Street, Winchester

They often visited her, sometimes staying for a day or two. As she grew more ill, her relations redoubled their efforts to please and help her. Cassandra was with her night and day: and Mary, James Austen's wife, forgot any ill feeling that had existed between her and her sister-in-law to come and assist Cassandra. The younger generation, too, showed affectionate concern. Fanny Knight wrote several times a week – her letters were a great pleasure to Jane – Edward sent inquiries from Oxford, young Charles Knight, still a boy at Winchester School, would look in and pay a short visit to Aunt Jane. Indeed the story of her last days illustrates the advantages of being a member of a united and affectionate family. It is also an advertisement for the values she and her world believed in. Good sense and good manners, humour and a firm religious faith – these stood Jane Austen in good stead on her deathbed.

Throughout the month of June, she lay or sat, gazing out from the little bow window of the College Street house at the changing Hampshire skies and leafy tree tops of Dr Gabell's garden. Then in the third week of July, her condition took a sharp turn for the worse. Informed by Dr Lyford, James and Henry told Jane that she had not long to live. She took the news calmly but asked if she might have the Sacrament administered to her while she was still able to realize its full significance and before her mind had begun to wander. She also spoke to those around her as if for the last time and taking leave of them. One remark she made is unexpected. To Mary Austen, James's wife, she said, 'You have always been a good sister to me.' 'Always' was a little strong; for till lately, she had never hesitated to say that she found Mary tiresome. But she was now so grateful to her for her kindness during the last weeks that she wanted every memory of past ill-feeling to be forgotten. The next day she unaccountably felt better; even well enough to compose a neat copy of verses, inspired by her amusement that St Swithin's Day, traditionally rainy, was also by custom the day of Winchester races. This poem, her last literary composition, proved to be a lightning before death. Cassandra, coming back the next afternoon from the town, found Jane in a faint. She came to but only to fall into another, which was succeeded by a brief period of suffering more acute than any she had endured before. For the only time in her illness, Jane's composure faltered. Cassandra asked her if there was anything she wished for: 'Only for death,' whispered Jane, 'God, grant me patience. Pray for me, Oh pray for me!' Within half an hour she became unconscious. At half past four on the morning of 18 July, still unconscious and with her head pillowed on Cassandra's shoulder, she died. Cassandra closed her eyes. Five days later she took a long last look at her much loved sister lying in her coffin, her features composed into an expression of serene sweetness. A calm settled on Cassandra's spirit to remain there when, on the morning of 24 July 1817, she watched from the window of the little house in College Street the funeral procession wend slowly out of sight on its way towards where Jane Austen was to be buried in the north aisle of Winchester Cathedral.

V

Jane Austen's life was so much a family life, she identified herself so much with the feelings and fortunes of her relations that it seems unnatural to say goodbye to her without first taking a look into the future to see what happened to them. Our curiosity is soon satisfied. The later life of the other Austens was undramatic, generally satisfactory and much what one would expect. Turning first to her mother and sister, we learn that Mrs Austen lingered on, an ageing invalid spending most of her time on her sofa but still cheerful and good-humoured. 'Ah my dear,' she said to her grandson Edward

Austen, 'you find me just where you left me on the sofa. I sometimes think that God Almighty must have forgotten me, but I dare say He will come to me in His own good time.' She died in 1827 at the age of eighty-eight.

Cassandra stayed on alone at Chawton, living largely in her memories of the past, surrounded by the same old furniture, reading the same old favourite books, sewing and teaching the village girls to read, as when her mother and sister were alive. The young Austens were to remember her as a white-haired old lady dressed in black satin, whose countenance, at the mention of her sister Jane, involuntarily lit up with a look of love. They felt it right to visit her from

Jane Austen's tomb in Winchester Cathedral

time to time and she received them kindly. But they could not help noticing that, without Aunt Jane, life at Chawton Cottage had lost its charm. Cassandra died in 1845. Young Edward Austen, with a touch of un-Austenlike romantic fancy, described her funeral.

> Charles Knight officiated . . . The day was fine, but the wind exceedingly boisterous, blowing the pall almost off the coffin, and quite sweeping away all sound of Charles' voice between the gate and the church door. It also struck me as remarkably emblematic of her age and condition that the wind whisked about us so many withered beech leaves, that the coffin was thickly strewn with them before the service closed.

One of her brothers had preceded Cassandra to the grave. James Austen, ailing for several years past, died suddenly only two years after his sister Jane, at the age of fifty-two. Edward Knight lived for twenty-six years more, passing prosperous uneventful days at Chawton and Godmersham, surrounded by troops of children and grandchildren. Henry Austen continued to be more entertaining but less successful than his brothers. After seeing to the publication of *Northanger Abbey* and *Persuasion*, he spent an unsettled life, partly at Steventon, and for some years in France, to end his days at Tunbridge Wells. In spite of his gifts as a preacher, he never managed to rise in his profession.

The same could not be said of his two sailor brothers. Handsome, pleasant, trustworthy and effective, they both rose steadily in the service to end their lives as admirals. Charles had the more adventurous career of the two, playing an important part in campaigns, first in the Middle and later in the Far East. There in 1852, on an expedition up the Irawaddy river, he was struck down with cholera and died 'winning all hearts', it was said, 'by his gentleness and kindness, when struggling with disease'. Jane Austen would have been pleased, but not surprised, by this tribute to her 'particular little brother'. Frank Austen, except for some years in command of the North American Fleet, spent less time at sea. His intelligence and decision of character led him to be employed at home, organizing and administrating. He did this so successfully that he finished his career even higher than Charles had done, showered with honours and Admiral of the Fleet. He died, the last of his generation, in 1865, aged ninety-one. His first wife had died young: later he had fulfilled his sisters' original wish and married, as his second wife, their dearest friend, Martha Lloyd.

What about the younger generation of the family, or rather what about those members of it who had been particular friends of Jane Austen? Again the answer is nothing unexpected – but for one disconcerting exception Jane's favourite niece, Fanny Knight. From her earlier history it is possible to infer – though her Aunt Jane did not – that she lacked humour and was perhaps a little foolish. Time was to discover in her character more disillusioning defects. Three years after Jane's death, Fanny married, for reasons unrecorded, Sir Edward Knatchbull, afterwards Knatchbull-Hugesson, a baronet eighteen years older than herself and with a grown-up daughter. By so doing, she had in her view gone up in the world; so much so as to make her look back patronizingly and with some embarrassment on what she saw as her obscure and provincial Austen relations; including even that Aunt Jane with whom, in the past, she had talked of passing 'delicious mornings'. In consequence she was a little put out in her old age – she lived till 1882 – to find that this same Aunt Jane had become a household word all over the English-speaking world and that she, Fanny, Lady Knatchbull-Hugesson, was now chiefly of interest to others as Jane Austen's niece. This, at least, is the only convincing explanation of a letter she wrote to one of her younger sisters.

Yes my love it is very true that Aunt Jane from various circumstances was not so refined as she ought to have been from her talent, and if she had lived fifty years later she would have been in many respects more suitable to our more refined tastes. They were not rich and the people around with whom they chiefly mixed, were not at all high-bred, or in short anything more than mediocre and they of course, tho' superior in mental powers and cultivation, were on the same level as far as refinement goes – but I think in later life their intercourse with Mrs Knight (who was very fond of and kind to them) improved them both and Aunt Jane was too clever not to put aside all possible signs of 'commonness' (if such an expression is allowable) and teach herself to be more refined, at least in intercourse with people in general. Both the Aunts (Cassandra and Jane) were brought up in the most complete ignorance of the World and its way (I mean as to fashion etc) and if it had not been for Papa's marriage which brought them into Kent and the kindness of Mrs Knight, who used often to have one or the other of the sisters staying with her, they would have been, tho' not less clever and agreeable in themselves, very much below par as to good Society and its ways. If you hate all this, I beg your pardon, but I felt it at my pen's end and it chose to come along and speak the truth.

The same words can mean different things at different periods; and I suppose what Fanny meant by Jane Austen's 'lack of refinement' was her eighteenth-century frankness in alluding openly to what, by Fanny's now Victorian standards of delicacy, were such unmentionable subjects as 'confinements' and 'kept mistresses'. Fate is a profoundly ironical spirit who could find even in Jane Austen a subject for sardonic amusement. In spite of all her penetrating insight, she never realized that the niece she loved best was in fact the one who appreciated her least; still less that she belonged potentially to a type of character she delighted to satirize.

There was no question of her other two nieces failing to appreciate her. Anna Lefroy felt her death so much that she could not go on writing her novel, it reminded her too painfully of her Aunt Jane and the pleasure she had discussing it with her. She threw the manuscript into the fire and, with tears in her eyes, watched it burn to ashes. But her memories of her aunt were less easily obliterated. Continuously she missed her; again and again she found herself noting some comic episode or personality and saying to herself, 'I must keep that for Aunt Jane', and then remembering that Aunt Jane was no longer there to hear about it. Her own later life was pitched in a minor key. Ben Lefroy, her husband, died young leaving Anna to get such happiness as she could from the companionship of her children and, like her aunt before her, from that of her nephews and nieces.

So even more did Caroline Austen. Indeed both her personality and her mode of life sound so like that of her Aunt Jane as to suggest that she modelled herself upon her. Though good-looking and lively with the Austen dark eyes and regular features, she never married but settled near her brother Edward of whom she was very fond; finding her chief interest in the life of his family in which she took an active part as the sympathetic friend and confidante of his children. She had a reputation, both with them and with her friends, of an admirable talker, quick-witted, fanciful, humorous and with an attractive gentle voice. For the rest, she read a great deal and wrote a little; but, with a horror of self-advertisement even greater than her aunt's, could never bring herself to send anything she wrote to a publisher.

There remains Edward. He too, but in its masculine manifestation, con- tinued the Austen tradition: so faithfully indeed that an account of his life and interests might seem to my readers like a repetition of earlier pages of this book. Like his grandfather he was a scholarly sociable country clergyman, who educated his children at home, largely by reading aloud to them; like his father and Uncle Henry, he wrote light verses and took part in private theatricals; like most male Austens, he enjoyed in his youth dancing and fishing and shooting. Lucky and possessed of a natural charm, he won the heart of his capricious great aunt Mrs Leigh Perrot who made him heir to her fortune. He was able with its help to lead a blameless and comfortable existence till his death at the age of seventy-one, liked and respected by his neighbours and – again like his grandfather – the centre of an unusually united and devoted family. So much amiability and respectability and good luck perversely inclines one to fancy him as a little insipid and conventional. In fact he was the most distinguished personality produced by the younger generation of the Austen family. His letters show that the quick civilized intelligence and warm responsive sweetness of nature, that had drawn his Aunt Jane to him as a boy of sixteen, remained with him all his life. He was also a born writer. In 1870 he wrote a memoir of Jane Austen built round his personal recollections of her. It is a charming little work of art, gracefully written and vividly evoking her personality. Edward Austen does not, it is true, tell us much about his aunt as author. But to do so would have been inconsistent with his purpose, which was to depict her as he remembered her and as she appeared to the people who knew her. Since throughout her life she had been at pains to hide her literary activities from the world, Edward had to confine himself to drawing Jane Austen the woman. In fact, the result is not so incomplete a portrait as might have been expected: for, as perceptive Edward realized, Jane Austen the author and Jane Austen the woman were essentially of a piece.

> Many may care to know [he wrote] whether the moral rectitude, the correct taste, and the warm affection with which she invested her ideal characters, were really existing in the native source whence those ideas flowed, and were actually exhibited by her in the various relations of life. I can indeed bear witness that there was scarcely a charm in her most delightful characters that was not a true reflection of her own sweet temper and loving heart. I was young when we'lost her; but the impressions made on the young are deep.

He added:

> Though in the course of fifty years I have forgotten much, I have not forgotten that Jane Austen was the delight of all her nephews and nieces. We did not think of her as being clever, still less as being famous: but we valued her as one always kind, sympathising, and amusing.

Let these last sentences end my pen portrait of Jane Austen. While engaged on it, I have come to like her so much that I want my farewell to be one that would have pleased her: and, surely, she would have been pleased by these words of Edward's. They keep her secret, shed no unwanted light on the hidden workings of her genius; and they praise her as she would have been glad to be praised. Indeed, and once again, they show her as exceptional. There are few great authors of whom they could have been written – even by an affectionate nephew.

Illustration
Acknowledgments

The producers of this book would like to thank all those who have given permission for pictures to be reproduced here.

COLOUR
The page numbers given are those opposite the colour plates.

Jane Austen's House, Chawton, Hampshire 128, 160, 176

Collection the great-grandsons of Admiral Sir Francis Austen (Photos: Angelo Hornak) reverse of frontispiece, 112 and front jacket

Reproduced by permission of the British Library Board 16, 88 (overleaf), 89

J. Butler-Kearney (photos) 128, 160

The Cooper-Bridgeman Library 16, 88

Ray Gardner (photos) 88 (overleaf), 89

Collection Edward Knight, Chawton House (Photo: Jeremy Whitaker) 129

Miss Helen Lefroy 161

The London Library 177

Victoria and Albert Museum, London frontispiece, 17, 113

Derrick Witty (photos) frontispiece, 17, 113, 176, 177

MONOCHROME
Abbot Hall Art Gallery, Kendal 11, 12

Collection David Astor (Photo: Sotheby Parke Bernet & Co.) 48

Jane Austen's House, Chawton, Hampshire 31, 35, 38, 39, 40, 53, 69, 70, 87, 109, 132, 133, 155

Collection the great-grandsons of Admiral Sir Francis Austen 22, 32, 137, 159, 194

Collection the great-great nephews of Jane Austen 57, 127

Reproduced by permission of the British Library Board 21, 29, 44, 91, 93, 94–5, 107, 130, 138

The Trustees of the British Museum, London 26, 52, 77, 96, 104–5, 114, 166–7

J. Butler-Kearney (photos) 35, 87, 133, 197

Crown Copyright. National Monuments Record 30

John Freeman (photos) 96, 104–5, 114, 166–7

Ray Gardner (photos) 91, 93, 94–5, 107

P.J. Gates (photos) 57, 127, 159, 194

Geoff Goode (photos) 54, 121, 184

Angelo Hornak (photos) 22, 32, 102, 137

Albert W. Kerr (photo) 199 ·

Collection Dorothy Langley Moore (Photo: Rainbird Library) 27

J.G. Lefroy, Esq. 74

The Raymond Mander and Joe Mitchenson Theatre Collection 168

The Mansell Collection 135

The National Galleries of Scotland 181

National Portrait Gallery, London 50, 51, 78, back of jacket

Victoria and Albert Museum, London 102

Jeremy Whitaker (photos) 31, 38, 39, 40, 53, 69, 70, 109, 132, 155

Index